JUSTICE
IN AMERICA

How it Works – How it Fails

BY RUSSELL F. MORAN

Coddington Press

PO Box 419

East Islip, NY 11730

Printed in the United States of America

ISBN-10: 1463632703

EAN-13: 9781463632700

To my wife Lynda,

for her love and patience

TABLE OF CONTENTS

CHAPTER 1

Introduction – What is Justice?

For over 20 years I interviewed lawyers and judges involved in civil jury trials. As founder and publisher of *The New York Jury Verdict Reporter* I had a bird's eye view of the battles waged in our courtrooms every day. I became fascinated by the interplay between judges and lawyers, litigants and expert witnesses, and the often startling results, both as a practicing lawyer and later as a journalist. It became clear to me that the profession of judging is unique in American life, and does not lend itself to comparisons to other occupations. It also became clear that the men and women of our judiciary lead a scary life; scary, that is, if they take their jobs seriously. Theirs is an occupation that affects the lives of people who come before them in profound and even life-changing ways.

Judges impact society in a way that is disproportionate to their numbers, because the field in which they labor – the law – guides, rules, and keeps us from the edge of chaos. There are about 51,000 judges of all types in the United States, including magistrates, arbitrators and mediators. There are some 1.2 million lawyers, about 22 per judge. Legislation, government regulations, and judicial decisions spawn complexity, and just as scientists and technologists help us negotiate the intricacies of the physical world, judges show us how to comport ourselves in the world of law. And sometimes they are wrong.

We are all familiar with the statue of Lady Justice that adorns courthouses across the land, either as a sculpture or a painted image. Lady Justice always has three recognizable features: she is blindfolded, manifesting her impartiality; she holds the "scales of justice," showing that she is ready to weigh competing claims; and she holds a sword, indicating that she means business. It's useful to keep Lady Justice in mind when thinking about the concept of justice.

Philosophers since Plato have been whacking away at the concept of justice like a piñata. The purpose of this book is not to dissect the various and changing concepts over the centuries, but to address the concerns of justice in a way that is familiar to any reader. Webster's captures the essence of the concept, and defines justice as "(t)he quality of being just; conformity to the principles of righteousness and rectitude in all things; strict performance of moral obligations; practical conformity to human or divine law; integrity in the dealings of men with each other; rectitude; equity; uprightness."[1]

Justice is often used as a synonym for the word "fairness." When someone says "that isn't fair," he often means "that isn't right," or "that isn't just." We make these judgments all the time, without thinking about it. If you're short-changed at the gas station, that isn't fair. If you see someone swipe an item from someone's shopping cart, that isn't right. These judgments don't require a philosophical analysis, or ponderous dissection of competing interests. Usually, you just know "it ain't right." Our concept of justice is deeply imbued with morality.

Justice is a human need, just as hunger or thirst, and a lack of justice results in a longing for it, as if one senses that something is missing – a "disturbance in the force." A longing for justice seems to be an innate human desire, not one formed by ideological opinions, although ideology can impact what one believes to be justice. A sense of justice or rightness lives in your gut, unless you are a sociopath, in which case you couldn't care less. A sociopath or a person suffering from an antisocial personality disorder is defined in the Diagnostic and Statistical Manual of the American Psychiatric Association as "...a pervasive pattern of disregard for, and violation of, the rights of others that begins in childhood or early adolescence and continues into adulthood."[2] If a normal person commits an act of injustice, he feels unsettled, perhaps ashamed or embarrassed, and although he may try to justify his actions in his mind, the very attempt at justification shows that he does care about his actions, and how they affect other people.. Don't expect justice from a sociopath.

A Single Act of Injustice that Started a Revolution

On December 16, 2010, a 26 year-old street vendor named Muhammad Bouazizi had set up his cart to sell produce in a rural town in Tunisia. He was approached by a woman municipal official who demanded to see his permit, which he didn't have and didn't need. According to witnesses, she slapped Mr. Bouazizi, confiscated his scale, and threw over his cart. He was also roughed up by police officers who accompanied her. He walked to the governor's office to complain, but the governor refused to see him. Shortly thereafter, he returned to the governor's building, doused himself with gasoline, and set himself on fire. That one act literally sparked a revolution to rival the European revolutions in 1848, and created an upheaval in the Middle East not seen since the fall of the Ottoman Empire. Subsequent protests led to the ouster of the Tunisian government and the exile of President Ben Ali barely a month after the incident. The revolution in Tunisia was soon followed by a revolution in: Egypt; a pending transfer of power in Yemen; a civil war in Libya; an uprising in Syria; major protests in Algeria, Armenia, Bahrain, Iran Iraq, Jordan, Morocco, and Oman; and minor protests in Azerbaijan, Djibouti, Kuwait, Lebanon, Mauritania, Saudi Arabia, Sudan, and Western Sahara. Collectively, these revolts are being referred to as the Arab Spring, although the history is still being written. And it all began with a single act of injustice, which galvanized people's thinking throughout the Middle East and North Africa. These protests and revolts were not the result of any single religious or ideological movement – they were the result of an outbreak of people longing for justice.

The Longest Wait for Justice in American History

On May 1, 2011, Osama Bin Laden was killed by an American SEAL team on a special military operation at the compound where he lived in Pakistan. The moving force behind the attacks of 911, and countless other murderous operations against innocents, Bin Laden eluded capture for almost 10 years. The past decade has seen a collective feeling of justice denied, not only among Americans, but among any civilized people. The visual display of the sheer joy that justice was delivered was seen from Times Square, to Ground Zero, to the National Mall, to cities and towns across the land. The vicious killer, who specialized in snuffing out the lives of innocents, came to a swift and brutal end. He was shot, killed, and buried at sea. Since 911 President George W. Bush spoke often that justice would eventually be done, and President Barack Obama was able to announce that justice finally had been done.

Distributive Justice

Distributive justice or economic justice is all the rage these days. This is the idea that the circumstances of life should not result in inequality, and the state should step in to level the playing field. The concept is all about the social justice of allocating goods in society. The late liberal political philosopher John Rawls is the leading proponent of this school of thought. In his book *A Theory of Justice*, Rawls held the view that "…each person is to have an equal right to the most extensive scheme of equal basic liberties compatible with a similar scheme of liberties for others" and that social and economic inequalities should be arranged so that the greatest benefit would flow to the most disadvantaged.[3] The idea of fairness is the essence of Rawls' thinking. He also posits the theory that we should get away from the idea that we deserve something, because when you analyze it we don't have a lot to be deserving of. Take, for example, a talented athlete who earns millions of dollars a year. Did he choose to have his talent, and therefore deserves our praise and his millions? Or did his genetic code give him his talent, and therefore should his riches be distributed more justly? The examples are endless: the inherited millionaire; the brilliant investment banker; the talented late night show host. What did these people do to deserve their advantage? They may have nurtured their talents, but their unearned innate talent has nothing to do with it. Rawls' theories are at the core of the debates between liberals, socialists, and Marxists on one side, and conservatives and libertarians on the other. The strict libertarian view holds that each life belongs to each individual, to conduct himself as he sees fit, so long as his actions do not cause harm to someone else. Rawls is a bit scary – it's hard to imagine how his ideas could be put to work, without the consent of the governed, except in a totalitarian state. This book is NOT about distributive justice. It is about the situations where a person we call a wrongdoer *affirmatively* does something bad to a person we call a victim, whether the wrongdoer commits a crime, a tort or breaches a contract. I'm not saying that distributive justice is something not worthy of discussing – it is – only that it is not the subject of this book.

But defining justice is the easy part. It gets difficult when we examine how different people view justice, and how they define a just result.

The following is a group of vignettes, most based on real facts. I ask you to determine if the facts indicate that justice has been done. If you feel uncomfortable after this exercise, relax. The object is to make you feel uncomfortable, and also to demonstrate that the elusive concept of justice isn't an easy one. I do not provide answers, because I'm not sure I have them.

Is There Justice in the Following Situations?

1. **Did the Defendant win by getting the death sentence?** Two men held a family hostage, including a mother, father, and two daughters, ages 11 and 17. They beat the father with a baseball bat and left him

for dead in the basement. He crawled to safety to a neighbor's house. The men took the wife to her bank to obtain $15,000. A bank security video was seen on national television which shows her advising the bank teller what is going on. You can't hear the woman, but her face is a graphic image of the word "fear." The teller alerts the police, but it is too late. The men sexually assault the wife and one of the daughters, then strangle them and set the house on fire. A jury returned a verdict on multiple counts against one of the men, Steven Hayes. His partner, Joshua Kimisarjevski will be tried in 2011. Hayes was sentenced to death. Now here's the rub: By all accounts Hayes *wants to die*, and was pleased with the verdict. Question: How do you punish a person who wants to die?

2. **Millions for the Lawyers – Pocket Change for the Clients.** A class action lawsuit was filed against Allstate and Farmers Insurance Companies over a practice called "double rounding." Under this method an insurer would "round up' a premium of, say, $1,000.50 to $1,001. The companies would then round again for semi-annual premiums. So $500.50 becomes $501, resulting in a driver paying $1,002 annually, or an extra $1.50 per year. The case settled. Each plaintiff-driver in the class got $5.50 (yes, five dollars and fifty cents), and the attorneys received a fee of $10.3 Million.[4] Nice work if you can get it! Was justice done here?

3. **Stoned to death for the offence of being raped.** A 13-year old Somali girl claimed that she was forcibly raped by three men as she walked to visit her grandmother. After her family reported the incident,

she was accused of adultery by local Islamist militants. She was sentenced to death by the most barbaric of methods – stoning. The sentence was carried out by dozens of men in a stadium packed with over 1,000 observers.[5] In a sane world, can this ever be called justice?

4. **50 years-to-Life for Shoplifting.** A guy stole five children's videotapes from a K-Mart, and 2 weeks later swiped another four videotapes from a different K-Mart. The retail value of the property was just over $150. His testimony was that he wanted the videos as Christmas presents for his nieces. He had a criminal record of petty crime going back a couple of decades. Under California's "three strikes" law, a third felony offense results in a mandatory minimum of 25 years to life. He was convicted of two felonies for the videotape thefts, nailing him with the third strike. He was sentenced to two consecutive 25-year- to- life sentences, making it 50 to life. The shoplifter, Leandro Andrade, will be eligible for parole in 2046 – when he is 87 years old.[6] Did Mr. Andrade receive justice?

5. **Taxpayer Funded Bonuses.** Insurance giant AIG received a massive taxpayer funded bailout of some $173 million during the financial crisis in 2008. Nevertheless, the company awarded over $165 million in bonuses to 418 employees, 73 of whom got over $1 million. The company defended the bonuses arguing that if it didn't honor its contract with the employees, they would flee for other ventures.[7] Ask a pink-slip recipient if this is justice.

6. **Price Gauging or Market Efficiency?** Nothing makes a politician happier than to call a press conference after a disaster, and accuse assorted villains of price gauging. After any major hurricane, there are always wide complaints of gasoline price gauging. But some argue that market forces should always be allowed to play out, and that higher prices insure that refineries will have the incentive to get the fuel to where it's needed, and that artificially low prices result in shortages. If the market was unable to assign higher prices, the market would then replace the high prices with scarcity. What is right?

7. **Is it Fair to be Born with a Silver Spoon in your Mouth?** Liberals believe that our institutions should strive to make things right for the downtrodden (see discussion of John Rawls above). Conservatives believe that an individual's best path to success is to let that person be challenged, and to use the challenges to forge a better life. On October 28, 1955, an African-American boy is born in a public hospital in a poor section of Brooklyn, NY. His parents are both drug addicts, and his father leaves the family when the boy is 3 years old. He misses school constantly and begins a career as a petty criminal when he is 15, and receives a 25 year sentence for armed robbery when he is 25. On the same day in Seattle, Washington, another boy is born. He is white, has educated and supportive parents who surround him with all the accoutrements of learning. The little boy from Seattle is named Bill Gates, and he becomes a gozillionaire. Ok, this example is about distributive justice, but I felt it belonged here as an example of what the debate is all about.

8. **What a difference a block can make.** On the same day, within a block of each other, two young men are severely injured in separate car accidents. One accident takes place in the Bronx, New York, and the other in Westchester County, which borders the Bronx. For the sake of this hypothetical, assume they are the same age, earn similar incomes, and sustain the same severe injuries. Each contacts a talented personal injury lawyer. A jury renders a verdict in Westchester, awarding plaintiff $95,000. Westchester, a wealthy area, is known among lawyers for its conservative jury verdicts. The Bronx, on the other hand, consists of working class neighborhoods, populated by potential jurors who tend to go for the underdog. and is known for its generous jury awards. The Bronx jury awards the other plaintiff $1,500,000. One block, big difference. Is it justice?

9. **How you are Injured can Make a Big Difference.** Similar to the above example, two young men are severely injured, one in car accident, the other by a physician who committed medical malpractice. In this example, the subsequent jury verdicts are in the same county, but in a state where there is a $250,000 cap on pain and suffering damage awards in medical malpractice verdicts. The car accident victim gets a verdict for his pain and suffering of $5,000,000. The medical malpractice victim gets $250,000. Same injury, big difference. Is this justice?

10. **A Compassionate Decision that Resulted in Tragedy.** In 2005 a Navy SEAL reconnaissance team was on a secret mission in Afghanistan near

the Pakistan border. They were seeking a high-value enemy target, a Taliban leader who commanded about 150 heavily armed fighters. Three goatherds and about 100 goats happened upon the team. The men trained their weapons on the herdsmen and motioned to them to sit down. They then debated about what to do – shoot them or let them go. If they let them go, chances were that the herdsmen would alert the nearby Taliban force, who would then attack the SEAL team. Petty officer Marcus Luttrell cast the deciding vote and they let the herdsmen go. About an hour and a half later they were attacked by the enemy force. Three of them were killed, and only Luttrell survived, although severely injured, by rolling down a hill and crawling seven miles to a friendly village. The Taliban force also shot down a helicopter that was attempting a rescue, killing all 16 aboard. Luttrell would later regret his vote to release the goatherds. "I must have been out of my mind. I had actually cast a vote which I knew could sign our death warrant."[8] With his vote, Lutrell showed compassion, but the result was hardly justice.

11. **It's Who you Know.** A woman accepted an exciting executive position with a fast- growing company. To take the job, she had to relocate her family and leave a secure well paying position. The day before she reported for work the vice-president who recruited her was fired. Her "political" position with the company was that of an outsider – she was considered one of "his" people. Instead of the large office she expected she was given a desk in a hall-way. The executive team that she looked forward

to working with was indeed a team – and she alone was the opposing team. Her dream of an executive career became the reality of being on overpaid functionary with no future. Inustice, or just the way the chips fall?

12. **Sometimes You Lose the Prize for the Wrong Reason.** A talented high school senior was everybody's bet to win the school's coveted Art History Medal. When she didn't win the award, she and many others were shocked. The essay was well written, extensive, and thoroughly researched. Years after graduation she would learn from someone on the committee that the reason she didn't get the prize was that her father was an artist, and the committee assumed that the essay was written by him. Truth is, he didn't even see the essay until after it was submitted. Can she forget this old injustice?

13. **He Would have Died Anyway. Is that an Excuse to Kill Him?** Four sailors were stranded in a lifeboat with little food and no water. One of them was a 17-year-old cabin boy. He drank seawater, became ill, and appeared to be dying. On the nineteenth day one of the men stabbed the boy to death. He and the other two ate the boy's remains. If they didn't eat, they all would have died. How would you judge them if they were in your courtroom?[9]

14. **Chloe – Get me CTU on the Phone!** Jack Bauer, the iconic star character in the long running TV series *24*, was not hesitant to use "advanced interrogation techniques," which some consider torture, when interviewing a suspect while a bomb is ticking. If the statue of Lady Justice was replaced by a statue

of Jack Bauer, you could eliminate the blindfold and the scales of justice – the sword is all that Jack needs. A member of the fictional CTU (Counter Terrorist Unit), Bauer would save civilization weekly by thwarting the bad guys, and would confront the audience with one of the major moral questions of the day: Is it just and moral to torture a suspect, when you know the suspect has knowledge of a ticking time bomb, and, if it detonates, hundreds of thousands of people will die? Khalid Sheik Mohammed, mastermind of the attacks of 911, was waterboarded – a process that replicates drowning – after his capture by American forces. He divulged information about a planned attack on Los Angeles. That attack was prevented because of the information he gave.[10] Opponents of torture argue that cruelty can never be justice. Those in favor stress the moral righteousness of saving countless lives. One of the tougher calls in moral philosophy.

The above stories only ripple the surface of the sea of moral issues that we face when discussing justice. For readers wanting to delve deeper into the philosophical aspects of justice, an excellent place to start is a book written by Harvard Professor Michael J. Sandel entitled *Justice: What's the Right Thing To Do?*[11] You should read this book not only for the challenge he poses to readers, but for the sheer joy of reading about a complex subject, written with such clarity that you think you're chatting with the author. Professor Sandel also delves into the writings on justice by Emmanuel Kant, Jeremy Bentham, John Stewart Mill, John Rawls, and Aristotle. His course at Harvard University, called *Justice*, is the most subscribed to course in the history of the university. The book is based on his lectures, which were turned into a 12-part TV series. You can view video excerpts of Professor Sandel's lectures at the website www.justiceharvard.org. It is worth your time.

To encounter justice and injustice, you need not read the newspapers and books. Think of justice in your life, of those times when you were treated unjustly or, perhaps, when you acted unjustly. This is a useful exercise, one which will make the rest of this book more meaningful for you. Think of your feelings, which probably bubble up when you recreate the incidents from your memory. Do you feel anger, hurt, remorse? What does your gut tell you about that time when you suffered a wrong that was not righted. Do you want to rebalance the scales, to do it over, to right the wrong? Do you want revenge? That last question is the emotional tipping point, because it goes to the very essence of why civilized nations have systems of justice. Imagine a country where the government basically said to you: "It's your problem – the state isn't going to help you." Such a country would be a barbaric and scary place, a place where justice is left for individuals to right their own wrongs. It would be a place of vendettas and constant violence, where the Hatfields and the McCoys are in a constant war of retribution. Such places, of course, do exist. Somalia, for example, has been without a functioning government for almost two decades. Have a problem? Don't call a cop. Recall that the previous example of the 13-year-old girl who was stoned to death for being raped happened in Somalia.

In a state without a system of justice you either seek your own justice or pay homage to a local warlord, who is actually a substitute for a functioning state. Citizens of Afghanistan, especially in its remote parts, often side with the Taliban because the central government is so weak and corrupt that the inhabitants have learned not to rely on it. They overlook the barbarity of the militants, because the militants at least bring some sense of normalcy to life, some predictability, some semblance of order. They are also very big on revenge. The mafia performed a similar function in Sicily and also in America during and after the great wave of Italian immigration in the last century. Immigrants who could not find justice through normal institutions found it through the local mafia boss, *the Don*. Recall the famous scene at the beginning of the movie *The Godfather* where an undertaker asked Don Corleone to punish some thugs for raping his daughter. Justice had failed him: the thugs had beaten the criminal charge, and even grinned at the man after their acquittal. Crying for revenge, he called the Don "Godfather" and kissed his ring, thereby paying a fealty, and signing up for an alternative system of justice.

In a modern state with a system of justice in place, you don't feel that you need to seek revenge because the state has an elaborate system of laws, which in some cases are even a means of revenge. Primitive as it may sound, the government does seek revenge through the punishment apparatus of the criminal law, albeit in an orderly and civilized way. Even in the civil law, a form of punishment may be meted out with punitive or exemplary damages, and even if punitive damages are not available, the law attempts to right the wrong, or to make you whole, by allowing for compensatory damages. Imagine some jerk runs a red light and smashes into your car, seriously injuring you. You don't seek revenge: you sue the bastard!

The Small Things in Life Add Up

The small injustices that we suffer leave us angry or frustrated, because they are just too small for us to seek a formal legal solution. The law may be on your side, but the expense of righting the wrong far outweighs the wrong. Attorneys are often frustrated when a potential client appears and tells them a story of an obvious injustice, but the remedy does not justify what the lawyer would have to charge. Put aside lawyer jokes for the moment and consider: the lawyer has to bill a certain minimum amount just to cover his overhead, not to mention put food on his family's table. Consider some of the following examples, many of which may have happened to you.

- When buying a new car, you initial a box on the paperwork that says the car has a full tank of gas. You leave the lot and drive off. Shortly before getting home, you notice that the tank is almost empty. You pull into a gas station and fill it up. The next day you call the dealer and explain. You are told that you can bring the car back and they will fill it up, which means that you will have to drive it till the tank is almost empty to get the bargain you thought you had. It's a $50 problem, so you forget about it. Or do you?

- A guy notices that his mileage is about to go over the limit on his lease, so he decides to pay the six remaining lease payments and get a new car. The dealer refuses to take the car back until the end of the lease – even though the lessee had paid up in full. So the car has to sit in his driveway, fully insured, for 6 months. Sometimes injustice results from stupidity.

- A couple wants to buy a leather ottoman to go with a new chair. They check the receipt which says: "sea green." They then take a picture to make sure. They go to the store, along with the picture and the receipt, and request a special order of a sea green ottoman. When it arrives, it is not even close to the color of the chair. The store refuses to take it back because it was a special order. A $175 problem. Anger, but no new ottoman.

- You buy a bunch of trees from a nursery for $1,000 and decide to plant them yourself to save the $300 planting fee. They all die within one season. You go to the nursery and are told that there is no guarantee because you planted them yourself. You ask the manager to check with the manufacturer to see if they are defective. The manufacturer's rep inspects the trees and discovers that they are indeed defective. The nursery manager promises you a credit, but it will cost you more than you initially paid because of a "replanting fee." Of course you can sue in small claims court, but you will need an expert witness – and a lot of time.

- About every other month you see a small charge on your credit card that you don't recognize. You call the phone number listed next to the item, and get a message that the phone is disconnected. You then try to access the website that is listed, and there is no such website. You call your credit card company and they readily correct the problem (credit card companies try to be good like that, to encourage you to use the card). So even though the problem went away, there is a lingering sense of injustice, which is regularly perpetrated on people who don't scrutinize their credit card bills. Little scams like this abound.

• You invite guests to your apartment for dinner. The guest parking space in the complex was covered with freshly plowed snow after a recent blizzard, so your guests ask you where to park. You check with management, and the guy on duty says to park anywhere – 80% of the spots in this resort community were empty in the month of January. Your guest picks a spot and parks. When they went to retrieve their car after dinner they found it had been towed. After an evening of embarrassment, aggravation, and a $140 impound fee, they learned that the owner of the marked spot in question had the car towed. Was this just? The owner of the parking space had the legal right to have the car towed – there were signs all over the place warning against unauthorized parking. But this was January, and there were empty spots all over the place. Sometimes it is wrong to exercise a legal right.

• Like you, I often receive an email, usually from a retired Minister of Whatever from Nigeria, stating, in very formal tones, that because of a sudden influx of cash he needs to wire it to an American bank account. He has chosen you, and to show his gratitude, he will give you a percentage fee amounting to $18,000,000. Wow – that should pay a few bills! All he asks is that you give him your bank account number, routing number, social security number, username and password. You should have the money by tomorrow afternoon. This is not an injustice, you say, because nobody could be so stupid as to fall for this con. Really? My friend, a

Foreign Service officer, once worked as consular official in the American Embassy in Lagos, Nigeria. He told me that about once a month some American would come to complain that his bank account had been wiped out by former Minister Whazhisname. Sometimes suckers are complicit in creating an injustice.

What is Right? What is Just?

Let's test our personal "justice muscle" with the following scenarios. I list them under three categories: easy, less easy, and tough. For each example I ask you to ask yourself:

A. Is this right? and

B. Can you pull it off?

Easy (at least I think these are easy). For each, ask yourself: A. Is this right? B. Can you pull it off?

- Help a person in need as best you can.

- Return a wallet that you found to its owner.

- Console a crying child.

- Pick up the newspaper for your vacationing neighbor, who forgot to hold delivery.

- Take in a lost puppy and try to find its owner.

- Call 911 when you see an accident.

- Vote in elections.

- Hold the door for an elderly person.

Less Easy – For each, ask yourself: A. Is this right? B. Can you pull it off?

- Help a person you really don't like.

- Console a crying child, who has just killed a rabbit.

- Return a wallet to a person whom you know to be a fraud.

- Pick up the newspaper for a neighbor who never talks to you.

- You see your ex-wife's divorce lawyer slip on ice and not get up. Call 911?

Tough – For each, ask yourself: A. Is this right? B. Can you pull it off?

- Help a person in need, even though he has just burglarized your house.

- Return a wallet to a person you know to be a drug dealer.

- Console a crying child who has just killed your dog.

- Pick up the newspaper for a neighbor who has recently sued you.

- You're out of work and your unemployment benefits have expired. You find a wallet with a large amount of cash in it. Contact the owner?

This book is not a cheery civics lesson where truth, justice, and the American way always win out. No, it doesn't always work out, and everyday wrongs are committed that are never righted, where bad guys get off and good guys are left holding the bag. Sometimes the evidence that would have guaranteed a just result got lost. Sometimes the heroic key eyewitness dies the day before trial. Sometimes the jury – or judge – simply makes a stupid decision. Sometimes it rains on your parade. A friend of mine with a great, if dark, sense of humor gave me a coffee mug for my birthday. It says: "Life's a bitch – then you die."

But we can make life a bit more just and moral for ourselves and others. It just takes some work.

CHAPTER 2

The Economic Meltdown

Basic to the concept of justice is that when it is breached, there is a victim. *A* did something bad to *B*, and therefore *B* becomes a victim. We'll call *A* simply a wrongdoer. If, on the other hand, bad things just happen to *B*, he may not be a victim at all, or if we still want to call him a victim he would be a victim of circumstances, not a victim of somebody's wrongdoing. I know a guy who owns a body and fender repair business. The motto painted on the front of his truck says it all: "Shit Happens." In the fall of 2008, it did happen, big.

I would guess that there are as many books about the Great Financial Meltdown of 2008 as there are diet books. There are talented financial journalists and some economists who are helping to assess the disaster, and their aggregate work may someday help us to avoid another one. As I write this book in the Spring of 2011 we are still shaking our heads and asking how this could happen. Unemployment hovers close to 9%, the housing market is still looking for a bottom, and poorly documented mortgage papers are making the matter worse. The Federal Reserve keeps interest rates at historic lows, but bankers treat loan applicants as if they were asking for human sacrifice. Employers, still reeling from their difficult layoff decisions, are extremely cautious about hiring new staff. State and municipal governments are facing the most difficult financial burdens ever. California, with an economy larger than France, is at the doorstep of insolvency because of diminished tax revenues and gigantic shortfalls in pension contributions caused not only by lower tax revenue but by unrealistic actuarial assumptions made years ago. Local governments rely heavily on transfer taxes on mortgages and on the transactions themselves. As the number of transactions drops precipitously, the revenues drop with it. Reduced real estate tax revenue, another major source of municipal income, also contributes to the strain.

Who did this? Only politicians seem to have no problem answering that question, and the answer they come up with is: "everybody but us politicians." They blame banks (*predatory lenders*) insurance companies, mortgage brokers, Wall Street in general, and investment bankers in particular. A lot of people blame former Fed Chairman Alan Greenspan for his persistent easy money policy. It's always a good idea to pick on a retired guy – that way nobody gets hurt. Bill O'Reilly blames Congressman Barney Frank (head of the House Banking Committee). Barney Frank blames the greedy bankers. The greedy bankers blame the rating services, who in turn blame the sheer complexity of the stuff they were rating. Everybody blames the hapless borrowers for letting themselves get into mortgages they could not afford.

Let's look at what happened. In the early to mid-2000s real estate was on a tear. Mortgage lending practices became so lax it's hardly proper to even call them practices. There was a time in America that there existed a thing called a "starter house." It worked like this. You scrape and save and find a small house for you and your growing family. The most attractive thing about the house is that you could afford it. Maybe it has two bedrooms and one bath, so the two kids double up in one of the bedrooms, and all await their turn for the bathroom.

It had a nice small yard that could be maintained with an inexpensive lawnmower, without the need for a gardening crew. As your income and family grew, you put the house on the market, to be purchased by someone else looking for a starter house, and you move up to something bigger, but still affordable. That all changed with the new millennium. Now, your starter house becomes your dream house. The basic requirement for qualifying for a mortgage in 2004 was that you had a pulse. "No-doc" (no documentation required) mortgages were all the rage, and a *stated income* mortgage application meant that you could simply lie about your ability to pay. These became known as *liar loans*. With a liar loan, you "state" your income and nobody checks. The mortgage instruments themselves contributed to the frenzy. The old fashioned 30-year fixed rate mortgage, where you would make a fixed payment of principal and interest over the years, was for sissies. Now you had the option to get an adjustable rate mortgage and could opt to pay interest only, or even a *negative amortization* payment. A negative amortization option meant that the amount you paid would not even be enough to pay the interest on the debt. But that's ok, as mortgage brokers across the land told applicants, if the rate adjusts up suddenly, simply refinance and you're in fine shape. We all heard those loose money commercials. "Real estate is red hot. Unlock the hidden money in your home's value and fix up the house, pay off some bills, or take that European vacation you've been thinking about." Home equity became the nation's ATM machine. Just jump on the "refi" gravy train and ride your way to bliss. A 20% down payment? You must be kidding me. Lenders were getting people into a house with zero down plus, say, another 6% to cover your closing costs, which meant that they were paying you to take the mortgage. The accelerating home values gave the lender the secure feeling they needed, a feeling once provided by a buyer's 20% down payment. So there occurred the bizarre circumstance that home buyers would have none of their own money at risk.

Risk is something that got handed off like a hot potato. Besides the homeowner having no "skin in the game," the lenders had little to worry about too. The mortgage broker? He gets his fee and moves on. The lenders? They sell the paper to a third party. Then the geniuses at the big financial institutions got into the game. I remember reading an article in 2006 in the New York Times Magazine about a thing called a "collateralized debt obligation."[12] This was one of those little financial beasties that contributed heavily to the problem. It's a financial instrument that was part of the practice of securitizing mortgages. Lehman Bros. and their ilk would buy up gazillions of mortgages and put them into a bond instrument and sell them as a security. The underlying mortgages provided the principal and the mortgage payments provided the income. Again, pass off the risk. A collateralized default obligation was a product that looked like an insurance policy, sort of. They weren't really insurance policies which are carefully regulated and require reserves against future losses. The problem was that nobody could understand these things because they were so complex. They were created by well-paid propeller heads, typically with a PhD in math or physics. These folks are known as quantitative analysts, or "*quants*."

All of this made ultimate sense, as long as one condition held: the real estate market must keep going up. If you're inside a bubble and look out, everything looks bright and clear, even clearer because bubbles amplify things.

Now let's have a reality check, dear reader. Let's go back to the early 2000s and recall what we were thinking. I think you will agree that in diners, bars, living rooms and kitchens across the fruited plain, we all agreed that these crazy real estate prices couldn't keep going up like they were. A few economists, and maybe even a banker or two, thought the same thing. You didn't need a calculator to figure out that in a few years, if the market held true, it would cost a million bucks to buy a dwelling in a trailer park. But what did we do about it? I know I made my contribution to the festivities by buying a waterfront condo in Newport, Rhode Island in late 2004 – at full asking price, of course, which was the only way to get a condo in that development. Being on the water, with a deeded dock as part of the deal, the units were usually on the market for 72 hours before they sold. The guy across the hall from me bought a few months before I did and "flipped" it at a 28% profit in 8 months. Flipping a property now seems like a quaint phrase from another time. We wanted to let the good times roll! A couple of years ago I put the condo on the market. In 18 months I didn't have one showing. I now realize that the strange noise I heard at the closing was the sound a roller coaster makes as it slows toward the top of the hill. I don't know anybody who didn't believe that the market was too hot; nevertheless, we all wanted in on the party. Bubbles are like that.

And now the next set of rogue waves are rolling toward shore. Lawyers, some of whom are volunteers, began to represent people facing foreclosure. Clawing through the paperwork, which is what a good lawyer does, some noticed that the documentation papers required for foreclosures were often signed by the same person. A little digging revealed that some bank employees who were signing off on the documents would process hundreds of them a week. Now, it takes some time and effort to document, to a court's satisfaction, that the necessary elements are in place to entitle a bank to foreclose. Is the first mortgage valid? Check. Have payments been defaulted on, and if so, exactly how much? Check. Are there any other liens that could stand in the way of the first mortgage? Check. This all takes some doing, and there is no way that the signer could review hundreds of documents a week. So we now have yet another new phrase from the financial crisis lexicon: "robo-signers." And this is no mere technicality – the law, and the mortgage papers themselves, do require diligent reading before a court can fork over a deed to the bank. All this new mess means is that the process gets slowed down to a crawl. It may be temporary good news to the debtor, but only temporary. If the payments have not been made the borrower will eventually lose the house, so the slow-down in the foreclosure process does nothing more than put off the inevitable. But, what happens in the meantime is that the whole cleansing process of selling off foreclosed properties grinds to a near halt, and the eventual recovery of the real estate market gets dialed forward. Why buy a house now when there are new foreclosures advertised every week? Even better bargains are just over the horizon! That's why the real estate market is stuck.

Looking for Victims in All the Wrong Places

Ok, back to justice. Let's look for some victims. The best place to look is a land called *Predatory Lending.* This is where politicians labor because the victims are poor downtrodden borrowers, and the predators are banks. There are more downtrodden borrowers/voters than there are bank executives/voters so the harvest is good indeed. The victim always has the same story which goes something like "Hey, what did I know?" If I were starting a magazine called *Predatory Lending Victims Weekly,* I've got just the perfect person for the cover of my first issue. This is a true story told to me by Bob Phillips, a friend and well-respected mortgage broker from Long Island. Attorneys often send clients to see Bob, not just as a referral, but for Bob to interview the person to see whether he could qualify for a mortgage, to vet the deal, so to speak. So up shows a guy in Bob's office with an attorney's Spanish-speaking legal assistant. The hopeful homeowner, let's call him Mr. Garcia, spoke not a word of English, and the attorney felt very uncomfortable about a mortgage that had been offered by another broker. He wanted Bob to counsel the borrower. After interviewing the borrower, Bob told him that he could not in good conscience recommend a mortgage to him, and tried his best to talk the guy out of going forward with the mortgage that he had been offered. Bob tried to convince him that he was not yet ready for home ownership. Bob suggested that the fellow rent as cheaply as possible, save up, and then buy a house he could afford – see discussion of "starter house" above. Mr. Garcia worked as a laborer at a local nursery. He thought he had found the perfect house and would hear nothing about passing up the deal. Here's what he was offered: a 106% no-doc mortgage (i.e., the bank would take his word for it about how much he earned) with a negative amortization payment of $600 per month less than the interest-only payment option. The mortgage was more than 100% because it included closing costs.

The borrower would have no skin in the game whatso-ever. The mortgage was adjustable of course. Even at the lowest payment option, his monthly payments would exceed his GROSS income. Bob told me that he felt sick that he was unable to convince this man that he was about to shove his financial future off a cliff. Mr. Garcia left Bob's office and bought the house with the crazy mortgage he had been offered. Bob told me that he heard through the grapevine that the deal did close, and the house was foreclosed within 3 years.

Was Mr. Garcia a victim of an injustice? Here was an unsophisticated man who couldn't even speak English getting involved in the biggest financial transaction of his life thus far. Was the other broker unscrupulous and just looking forward to getting his fee and moving on? I don't know the other broker, and neither did Bob, but I bet his thinking was not that of a predator or the agent of a predator. I bet his thinking was that he was giving this guy a shot at the American dream, and, like most real estate party animals in mid-decade, thought that if the payments got too tough, the borrower could always refinance. If Mr. Garcia was a victim, we need to look at what he lost – a victim always loses something, other-wise he's not a victim. Remember, this was a zero-down mortgage; Mr. Garcia put no money into the deal. Yes he did lose the house in foreclosure, but as Bob Philips tried to explain to him, he was not financially ready to buy a house anyway. The only thing he really lost was his credit rating. But with a no-doc mortgage, do you think maybe he fibbed a bit about his financial posi-tion? There are millions of Mr. Garcias across the coun-try. Newspapers across the land are fond of publishing human interest stories of Mr. and Mrs. America from the heartland, about to go through the agonies of foreclosure. Complete with photographs, the stories indeed tug at one's heartstrings. But the point is usually the same, at least in the *New York Times*: these people are victims, not participants complicit in the transaction that led to the problem. It's a sad thing when anybody loses a home to foreclosure. These are people who bet and lost, and now they suffer. But are they at fault by not exercising personal responsibility? Are they victims? Some have lost their homes because they lost their jobs and simply had no way of making mortgage payments, even if these folks were prudent and borrowed only what they could handle. With no income there is very little one can handle. But if they are victims, who are the wrongdoers?

In some states, like New York, it is customary for both the buyer and seller to hire their own real estate attorneys to handle the transaction. Some lawyers look at a real estate deal as a perfunctory matter, and that their job is to make sure the title is good and there are no outstanding liens, but the title company performs much the same service. But the role of a lawyer should be viewed as a traditional one – to look out for the client's best interest. During the real estate bubble, how many attorneys actually inquired whether their client could afford the deal? Many years ago, way before the real estate bubble, when I was a neophyte lawyer, I got a valuable lesson from a local friend and lawyer who showed me what it really means to represent a client. I represented the seller of a house that had an assumable mortgage. A buyer came along who had to funds to pay the difference between the existing mortgage and my client's asking price. The buyer, a recent widow, was new to the area and asked me for a referral to an attorney. I recommended my friend, Frank Johnston, a local guy with lots of real estate experience, who has since passed away. It looked like it would be a very simple deal, with no complications over obtaining a mortgage because it was assumable. We met in Frank's office, and he said he wanted to speak to his new client privately. After a few minutes, Frank and the prospective purchaser came back into the room and Frank announced that the deal could not happen. When he interviewed the client (who I had referred to him) he found out that even though the mortgage was assumable, the woman would have a very difficult time making payments, and the balance that she intended to put down was basically her nest egg, the remaining liquidity that she had after the passing of her husband. So here was a deal that should have been simple, at least from my point of view and that of my client the seller. But Frank shot the deal down. What he did was look out for the interests of his client. He prevented her from becoming a "victim." If there were more Frank Johnstons in the world there would be fewer victims.

If there are any wrongdoers in this mess it's you, me, Barney Frank, Alan Greenspan, Fannie, Freddie – all of us. In a bubble, the animal spirits take over, and we all get zoned out, thinking that, well, maybe it won't continue, but it sure is fun. In the late-'90s during the dot-com bubble, you could do no wrong by putting your money into an internet penny stock where the company didn't even have a business model. I recall Lawrence Taylor, the NY Giants football great, coming out with a company that was somehow going to sell some type of clothing over the Internet. Ok, what? To whom? How? Those were the days! Shortly after the dot-com bubble burst, we were ready for another one – real estate. Who ever said we are a rational species?

Can a Black Swan Cause Injustice?

Some consider the real estate collapse and financial crisis to be Black Swans. In his book *The Black Swan, The Impact of the Highly Improbable*, Nassim Nicholas Taleb describes a black swan as an unexpected event of great impact, which is later rationalized by many who think that it was really foreseen.[13] Among such events he includes the founding of Google and the 911 attacks. The book has a great name. When you think of a swan, you always think it's white. Have you ever seen a black swan? I haven't either. So if you see one, you freak out, because that's just not the way things are supposed to be. Think of a black swan as: "What the hell is that and where did it come from?" So, was the real estate crash, the financial and credit crisis, and the whole general mess at the end of the decade black swans? We certainly did freak out, but it seems to me that the warning signs were so clear that we should have seen it coming.

Tulip Mania – The Original Economic Bubble

The real estate bubble of the early 2000s followed closely on the heels of the dot-com bubble of the late 1990s. Will we ever learn? Probably not. In 1637 in Holland, tulips – yes the flower – became the object of a speculative frenzy. This became known as *Tulip Mania* or *Tulipomania*. The prices of the bulbs began to sky-rocket, aided by an early version of a derivatives market, where an investor would buy futures contracts on bulbs not yet planted. At one point the price for a single bulb exceeded the annual income of a skilled craftsman by 10 times.[14] And, as with any speculative bubble, the prices eventually crashed. Although it has become a subject of debate among economists as to just how severe the tulip mania was, the story nevertheless stands as a metaphor for speculative excess.

It's getting tedious listening to politicians carping about victims. A victim means a heartbreaking story, and a heartbreaking story means a press conference, and a press conference means valuable vote-getting face-time for the politician. Remember the great Mighty Mouse: "Here I come to save the day!" Mighty Mouse would feel comfortable in Congress. These trying times are less about injustices and predators and victims, and more about a nation of people who didn't want to hit the slow button. We were all too busy enjoying the party that we didn't notice the house was on fire.

So while the newspapers and TV specials talk about the injustice of this mess – and a story about Mr. and Mrs. Jones from Dubuque who are facing the loss of their home makes for compelling copy – the truth is a lot more complicated.

In the next chapter we will begin to see how the American legal system handles the issue of justice.

Meanwhile, I'm putting my money in tulips.

CHAPTER 3

The American System of Law

This chapter is an overview of the American legal system and how it attempts to deliver justice. Entire textbooks, even treatises, have been written on this subject, so a comprehensive analysis is not intended. But huge subjects often boil down to certain fundamental principles, doctrines, and histories. Indeed, every law book in every law library could be summarized with these words: "Do good and avoid evil." All the other stuff is just detail. It is in that spirit that I invite you to read this chapter.

Ignorance of the Law

The most basic principle of the legal system is this: *ignorance of the law is no excuse.* We are all presumed to know all of the cases, statutes, rules, and regulations lining the walls of law libraries. Do we really know that stuff? Of course not, and that includes lawyers, judges,and law professors, but no legal system can function if a defendant were able to plead: "I'm sorry your honor, but I was simply unaware of that law." Knowledge of the law is a legal fiction that makes the entire system work. In New York City, for example, you cannot make a right turn at a red light. You cannot argue that you are from the suburbs and didn't know that local statute. You are presumed to know it as soon as you cross the city line. Try telling a cop that you haven't had the chance to review the local vehicle and traffic laws. Cops enjoy a good laugh.

Civil and Criminal Law

Derived from the English common law, also known as judge-made law, the American system of law incorporates the old common law principles, but also has adopted many of the characteristics of the European code system, where a legislature tries to cover all of the legal issues by passing laws. Legislation at all levels of government, combined with caselaw, and then mixed in with administrative law from the various agencies of government at federal, state and local levels has given us a complex quilt of legal mandates around which we must maneuver. The broad distinctions of criminal and civil law often overlap, and, occasionally, conflict.

Civil Law

The broadest division in our justice system is between civil law and criminal law, and the two differ significantly. In a civil dispute a plaintiff (the one with the gripe) sues the defendant seeking either money damages or "equitable relief," that is, asking the judge to tell the defendant not to do something (a Temporary Restraining Order – TRO, or an injunction) or to do something (mandatory injunction or a mandamus). A common civil dispute involves the commission of a tort. A tort is a civil wrong, or more specifically, a breach of a civil duty that you owe to someone. You and I owe each other a lot of duties, including the duty no to punch each other in the nose, not to trespass on each other's property and not to drive like a nut and negligently inflict injury. A tort may also be a crime. For example, if you punch someone in the nose, you have committed a tort for which you may be sued. You also have committed the crime of battery, for which you may be criminally prosecuted. You have breached a civil duty to the individual, as well as a societal duty that the law has forbidden. In tort law there is one overarching principle: We are all expected to act *reasonably under the circumstances*. Jamming on your brakes in traffic might be unreasonable if you do so to answer your cellphone. It might be reasonable if a pedestrian darts out in front of you. Torts make up the greatest volume of cases in our court systems, and are treated more extensively in Chapter 12.

A civil case begins with a "complaint" delivered to the defendant, usually by a person known as a process server. Defendant then has a strict period of time to "answer" the complaint, typically 30 days. Once the answer has been sent to plaintiff, the lawsuit is on. Then begins a process of "discovery," in which defendant is entitled to find out the evidence that plaintiff possesses. Modern discovery rules take much of the mystery out of a lawsuit, and help the system to get at the truth by forcing each side to show its hand. Discovery can be in the form of questions on paper (interrogatories or a bill of particulars) or by personal appearance (deposition or examination before trial). Whether on paper or in person, all parties giving information are sworn by oath and are under the penalty of perjury. A note on perjury: the law frowns upon it, to say the least. Lying under oath is not something you want to do, and you can and will go to jail if found guilty. So when you "promise to tell the truth, the whole truth, and nothing but the truth" – do it! Throughout the life of a lawsuit there may be many "motions" by either party. A motion is a request for an order, usually supported by legal arguments addressing some issue in the lawsuit. There are also "preliminary hearings," where the attorneys appear before the judge to address various matters involving the case. There are also both formal and informal "settlement conferences," where both sides see if a settlement can be reached before trial.

Both parties stand to benefit from a settlement rather than hazard the large financial burden of a trial, not to mention the risk of losing. The judge and the entire judicial system also benefit from a pretrial settlement because it means one less case on the docket, absorbing time and resources. Once a settlement is reached, it ends the case. You can't come back into court and say that you have had second thoughts. No, it is an agreement, and is enforceable. Mark Zuckerberg, the founder of Facebook, was sued by the Winkelvoss twins, college classmates of his at the time of the company's founding. The lawsuit was a major part of the motion picture *The Social Network*. They claimed that he had stolen their idea. The suit settled in 2008 for approximately $65 million. The twins went back to court and sued to set aside the settlement, claiming that they were misled by Facebook on the true valuation and that the proper valuation in 2008 should have been more like $120 million. They lost the case and also the appeal. The court noted that these were two highly educated people represented by experienced lawyers and financial advisors. The only time you are likely to see a settlement set aside for reconsideration is an opposite set of facts from the Winkelvoss twins. If a person of meager education, who was poorly represented, and especially if the other party lied, then, and only then, might you see a settlement reopened.

If a settlement cannot be reached, the case must go to trial, either before a jury or before the judge alone (bench trial). The jury, or the judge in a bench trial, is known as the "finder of fact." The United States Constitution provides for a right to a jury trial in certain civil cases. The Seventh Amendment states: "In Suits at common law, where the value in controversy shall exceed twenty dollars, the right of trial by jury shall be preserved, and no fact tried by a jury, shall be otherwise re-examined in any Court of the United States, than according to the rules of the common law." Note that the Constitution says "Suits at common law." In many types of lawsuits there is no right to a jury trial, such as patent law cases, federal and state court of claims cases (lawsuits against the government) and many others, because these cases arise out of a statute, not common law (judge-made law). Twenty bucks went a long way in the eighteenth century, but nobody has sought to amend the Constitution to raise the threshold, so jury trials are likely to be around for a long time. The common law is discussed below.

Whether it's a jury trial or bench trial, it is an expensive way to resolve a dispute. A trial is often referred to by lawyers as a "bonfire of cash," And a reputable litigator should forwarn his client of the perils ahead. In a corporate lawsuit, the legal fees can be staggering. Litigation over a major issue, such as a patent violation, requires the review of thousands of documents, both paper and electronic. Every email sent over a period of time must be checked for damning (or exculpatory) evidence. Picture a gymnasium lined with rows and rows of tables, each manned by lawyers billing by the hour. In cases where expert testimony is required, the numbers tick up even more. In a medical malpractice or product liability trial, for example, an expert witness or witnesses are required by law, because a juror is not able to make a decision, as a layperson, whether the doctor was negligent, or a product was designed with a defect. These are questions "outside the scope" of the jury. In a jury trial, the judge instructs the jury on the law (charges the jury), telling them, among other things, that they must decide based on the *preponderance of the evidence*. The best way to understand this is to think of the scales of justice: the preponderance of evidence tips the scales one way or the other. This is the legal standard that juries must use to decide the outcome of a civil lawsuit. Although judges may discuss or emphasize certain facts, they cannot tell the jury how to decide. But, if a jury comes back with a verdict that obviously ignored the evidence, the judge can set aside the finding of fact *as a matter of law*. Once the finder of fact reaches a verdict, the result is a judgment, which becomes a formal document. Typically there are motions made at the end of the trial. Some post trial motions include a motion to set aside the verdict as against the weight of the evidence, a motion for a new trial, or a motion for leave to appeal. The last one is very important. Once the trial is over and the judge does not grant any other motions, the only recourse for a losing party is to appeal to a higher court, assuming there is any money left after the cash bonfire of the trial.

Criminal Law

In the criminal law system, the plaintiff is replaced by a prosecutor, a public official such as a district attorney or state's attorney, who represents "the people," and whose objective is to punish the defendant by sending him to jail, or to fine him. The United States Constitution guarantees the right to a jury trial in a criminal case. The Sixth Amendment states:

> In all criminal prosecutions, the accused shall enjoy the right to a speedy and public trial, by an impartial jury of the State and district wherein the crime shall have been committed, which district shall have been previously ascertained by law, and to be informed of the nature and cause of the accusation; to be confronted with the witnesses against him; to have compulsory process for obtaining witnesses in his favor, and to have the Assistance of Counsel for his defense.

In the criminal law, if a statute doesn't prohibit something, it is not a crime, simple as that. There is no common law (judge made law) that can create a crime where the legislature has not passed a statute on the issue.

A criminal case begins either with an indictment or a document known as a "criminal information." Grammatical purists may scoff at the use of the modifier "a" in front of the word information, because information is a noun that cannot be counted or divided. It could have been called an Information Document or a Writ of Information, but it's not. Live with it. A criminal information is simply a document filed by the prosecutor that sets forth the charges against defendant. An information can be used if defendant waives his right to have a grand jury weigh the evidence against him. An indictment or an information amount to the same thing: a list of the charges that the prosecutor accuses defendant of having committed.

Bernard Madoff, the King of the Ponzi schemers, was not indicted, but was accused in a criminal information after he waived his right to a grand jury. Indictments are decisions made by a grand jury. A grand jury comes from the same pool of citizens as a regular jury (*petit jury*), and sitting on one can be anything but grand. A grand jury convenes for sessions over a relatively long period of time, as long as 36 months in the federal system. It's like having a lengthy, and very low paying, part-time job. The grand jury does not determine guilt or innocence, but only whether a person *should be charged* with the crimes that the prosecutor claims. The prosecutor does not have to prove his claims beyond a reasonable doubt in the indictment, but only that a reasonable suspicion or probable cause exists to try the defendant. At this stage, defendant does not have the right to call witnesses or even to be present, which means that the deck is stacked in favor of the prosecution at this point. Former Chief Judge of the New York State Court of Appeals Sol Wachtler famously observed that a prosecutor could get a grand jury to "indict a ham sandwich."

After a person has been indicted or served with a criminal information, he is brought before a judge for *arraignment*, a proceeding where he is advised of the allegations against him and asked to plead guilty or not guilty. F. Lee Bailey, world famous criminal lawyer, says that "not guilty" really means "prove it." This is the best way to understand the pleading – "I'm saying I'm not guilty – Unless you can prove it." The defendant may be released on bail or put into custody until a bail hearing takes place. In a criminal case, a jury must find the defendant guilty by unanimous vote. Civil trials vary from state to state, but may not require unanimity.

A crucial difference between civil and criminal law is the *standard* that the jury must use to render its verdict.

In a civil lawsuit, as discussed above, the standard of proof is a ***preponderance of the evidence***. In criminal cases, the standard to find a defendant guilty is ***beyond a reasonable doubt.*** The state must prove that defendant committed the crime beyond a reasonable doubt, or defendant walks. The drama of this was splashed on TV screens the world over at the end of the OJ Simpson murder trial. After the jury found defendant Simpson not guilty, Judge Ito gave a simple order: "Release the defendant from custody."

Jurisdiction

A court cannot hear a case before it unless it has *jurisdiction*, which is best understood as *power or authority*. There is *personal jurisdiction*: the court must have the power or authority to call a person before it. For example, a Connecticut court cannot hear a case against a defendant in California, unless the defendant was extradited by California in a criminal case, or consented to jurisdiction in a civil case. In contract matters, the question of jurisdiction is solved right in the document itself, where both parties agree to the jurisdiction of the state named in the contract. There are exceptions to this, as we will see shortly in the discussion of federal courts.

The second type of jurisdiction is *subject matter jurisdiction*. A court must have the power to allow a particular case to come before it. When I was a municipal attorney, our office was once served with papers about a lawsuit contesting real estate taxes on a taxpayer's property. The taxpayer represented himself. The suit demanded that the town appear in the local district court, a lower level court system in Nassau and Suffolk counties in New York. Problem is, the only court that has jurisdiction over property tax complaints (also known as tax certiorari suits) was the state supreme court. To save the gentleman time, I called him to let him know that he had filed in the wrong court. He would hear nothing of the sort, and demanded that the town appear to defend his claim on the date indicated. This was the easiest matter I ever handled. I simply appeared and advised the judge that his court had no jurisdiction over the matter, an opinion that the judge readily agreed with. I also advised the judge that I had tried to convince the taxpayer of his error. The guy then told me and the judge that he wanted to cost the town money by paying my salary for the court appearance, an argument of dubious logic, in that his gripe was that his taxes were too high. Fortunately for the taxpayer, the judge was a mild mannered soul, and didn't fine him.

Jurisdiction is jurisdiction – a court either has it or not. Some courts are known as courts of *general jurisdiction*. In all states there is one type of court that has the authority to hear almost any type of case. In the state system, these courts are often known by different names, often called a *superior* court. Courts of limited jurisdiction cannot hear cases that do not fit into their limited area of power. For example, a federal Admiralty Court cannot hear cases involving anything but cases involving maritime law.

The Supreme Court of the United States – Judicial Review

The Supreme Court of the United States consists of nine Justices appointed by the President and confirmed by the Senate. The Judicial Branch, including the Supreme Court, was established by Article One of the United States Constitution. The Constitution does not specify how many Justices shall sit on the Court, but the present number was set by the Judiciary Act of 1869. The Court decides cases arising under the United States Constitution and under federal law. Justice Scalia has estimated that less than one-fifth of the Supreme Court's decisions actually involve Constitutional issues – only one twentieth if you exclude criminal cases – but rather the interpretation of federal statutes and regulations.[15] The Constitution did not specifically give the court the power to rule on legislative acts, although many viewed such a power to be a logical component of the constitutional framework. The actual power of judicial review came about in 1803 in the historic case of *Marbury v. Madison*.[16] The case involved a simple matter. Marbury was appointed to the office of Justice of the Peace by the President, but his actual written commission was not delivered. He petitioned the Supreme Court to order Madison, the Secretary of State, to deliver the document, pursuant to the Judiciary Act of 1789. The court refused, holding that the act was unconstitutional. This was the first time that the Supreme Court held a congressional act unconstitutional, and gave birth to the doctrine of judicial review.

Lower Courts and Appellate Courts

Trials are conducted before a judge in a lower court. It changes from state to state, but lower courts may have names like district court, court of common pleas, superior court, circuit court, or, to completely confuse matters, in New York State the basic trial court is known as the supreme court. The reason for this is that in New York's supreme court system, these courts (there's one in each county, sometimes with multiple branches) have very broad general jurisdiction or power to hear pretty much any kind of case. But that goes for superior courts or district or circuit courts nationwide. But New York has to be different – the lower court is called *supreme*. Most of us mortals, including New Yorkers like me, think that the word supreme means the highest, the top banana, the big enchilada, the ultimate, the top of the line. Not in the Empire State.

So, trials get heard in lower courts in a courtroom presided over by a judge. Some trials are called bench trials and are heard by a judge without a jury. In such a case the judge is both the finder of fact and the decider of the law. In a jury trial, it is the jury's job to act as the finder of fact and the judge's job is to apply the law. At the end of a trial the judge issues an order, which can sometimes be a judgment for money damages. The loser can, and almost always will, make various motions (for a new trial, to set aside the verdict, etc.). If the post trial motion is denied, the losing party must "appeal" the judgment of the lower court, and appellate courts are where a disappointed party goes to try to reverse the lower court result. There are often layers of appellate courts, an intermediate appellate court and one court sitting as the state's highest court, usually known as a state Supreme Court (It is called the Court of Appeals in New York – don't ask). Once a party has exhausted his appeals in the state courts, he can appeal to the United States Supreme Court. It is extremely difficult to bring a case before the US Supreme Court, because it accepts only a very few cases each year, and those are cases of major importance. In the 2007 term, the Court only heard an historic low of 70 cases. Back in the 1980s it heard as many as 150 per year. The average is now about 80 cases out of 8,000 applications (petitions for a *writ of certiorari*).[17] The Supreme Court law clerks, those bright young people from the nation's top law schools, spend vast quantities of their time reviewing petitions for writs of certiorari. Over the last two decades, the Supreme Court has gotten very picky about the cases it wants to decide. You will often hear a disgruntled litigant say "I'll take this case all the way to the Supreme Court." To be accurate he would add "…If they agree to hear it."

Federal Courts

Federal district courts are the trial courts of the federal system, and they are easy to spot. Unlike the marble columned edifices of the state courts, federal courthouses tend to be steel and glass affairs, identifiable as a federal courthouse by the words on the front – "Federal Courthouse.." The federal courthouse in Central Islip on Long Island, for example, is a gigantic white structure, designed by the renowned architect Frederick Meyer. Because it is on federal property, there was no need to clear anything with the local zoning authorities. There was no attempt to blend the structure with local architecture or topography. It can be seen from space.

There are 94 Federal district courts in the country, and they hear both civil and criminal cases. Some have more than one courthouse, such as the Federal District Court for the Eastern District of New York, located in Brooklyn and Central Islip on Long Island. For a case to be brought in a federal district court there must be a federal question, that is, an issue involving federal law. Another type of case heard in the federal district courts are *diversity of citizenship* cases. This means that a case arose between a citizen of one state against a citizen of another. The framers of the Constitution were concerned that a jury in one state would favor its fellow state resident against the out-of-stater. The Constitution authorized Congress to allow jurisdiction in such cases, which it did in the Judiciary Act of 1789. Diversity cases, as they are called, are controversial to say the least. Many scholars and judges have long railed against opening the federal courts to these cases, arguing that it is an anachronistic holdover from agrarian times when people in one state would "root for the home team." A simple motor vehicle accident case can wind up in federal court if one of the parties is a citizen of a different state. There is nothing "federal" about it. In 2007 *almost one – third* of the 258,000 cases filed in the United States District Courts were based on diversity of citizenship – 28%.[18] Interestingly, 17% of the diversity cases filed were asbestos-related suits.[19] But, as anachronistic as it appears – it's in the Constitution.

Appeals in federal cases are heard by Federal Circuit Courts of Appeals. There are 13 federal Circuit Courts of Appeals in the United States. Eleven of them are defined by geography, including the D.C. Circuit, and one is called the United States Court of Appeals for the Federal Circuit, which has national jurisdiction but is limited to certain cases involving federal law subject matter. There are also federal appellate courts with limited jurisdiction such as the United States Court of Appeals for Veterans Claims or the United States Court of Appeals for the Armed Forces.

Small Claims Court

In all states there is a judicial institution usually called a small claims court. This is a great American tradition, one that delivers justice every day. These are real courts involving real controversies, albeit no large disputes. Some courts of limited jurisdiction will have a small claims day when these cases are heard. Some states have small claims courts where that is the court's only function. Designed so that the services of an attorney are not needed, the job of small claims court comes with its name – small claims. There is a limited amount of money that can be recovered, usually $10,000. The necessary documents are not complicated, the procedures and rules of evidence are not as strict as in a regular court, and decisions are often rendered on the spot. One of the unique features of small claims courts is that the court employees are trained to assist the litigants and are ready to answer any question. In Chapter One I discussed the small injustices of life and how they add up. Small claims court enables these small injustices to be made right. Even if a lawyer charges you a bargain basement fee, it's impossible to get restitution for a wrong that has cost you a small amount of money simply because the legal fees will chew up whatever you collect. Small claims court removes that obstacle.

Alternative Dispute Resolution – A Private System of Justice

Alternative dispute resolution, often referred to as ADR, is a private system of justice that is based on an agreement by parties to be bound by the decision. Most of the cases are arbitrations, but may also be mediations. Arbitrations begin with an agreement to be bound by the decision. Mediation is sort of a refereed settlement discussion, without a binding decision at the end. Many contracts have specific arbitration clauses in them, usually stating that any dispute will be heard by the American Arbitration Association, the granddaddy of ADRs. This shadow system of justice has very few critics, and it is becoming increasingly accepted by the legal profession and the general public. A large part of the popularity of ADRs is a result of the increasingly crowded court calendars, and the increasing time to get a case heard. A matter may be resolved within weeks or months, not years, when in front of an ADR company. The arbitrators are usually of a high caliber; often, retired judges will go to work for an ADR company. Parties go to mediation after signing a contract, which typically includes a provision where the parties agree to be bound by the decision. It may include a clause allowing for appeal. If a party refuses to accept the arbitrator's decision, the case becomes one for the traditional court system, based on breach of contract. Expect to see a constant growth of alternative dispute resolution.

The Common Law

We all learned in civics class that American law is based on the Common Law of England. The common law consists of decisions by judges, rather than laws written in statutes or decisions of administrative agencies. Under a common law system, a judge is bound by decisions of prior courts, which are now *precedent* for future decisions. This is the principle known as *stare decisis*, which comes from the Latin phrase "*Stare decisis et non quieta movere,"* which, in translation, means: "Maintain what has been decided and do not alter that which has been established." In other words, judges are not free to make it up as they go along, working from gut feelings. The Common Law may be defined simply as a *body of precedent*. When a case is before the court, the judge must follow decisions from other cases that have grappled with similar issues. If a case is *one of first impression,* meaning that no prior court has addressed the issue, the judge can then establish a new precedent. Lawyers in a common law system *find* the law by researching cases that have addressed an issue similar to the one facing their client.

The above paragraph is, of course, an oversimplification. In the United States we have a huge body of statutes, laws made by legislators, as well as a vast body of administrative law, which are usually rules and regulations made by administrative bodies such as the Environmental Protection Agency. Congress gives administrative agencies the power to pass regulations with the rule of law; otherwise legislators would not have time to sleep. Say, for example, Congress passed a law that nobody can chew gum on the National Mall, and passes simultaneously enabling legislation naming the Department of the Interior as the regulating body to enforce the law. That would probably result in a couple of volumes of regulations aimed at preventing you from chewing gum on the Mall. In the federal system the rules and regulations of administrative bodies are found in the Code of Federal Regulation (CFR). It takes up over 25 feet of library shelf space and grows every day, but this is not about to put judges out of business. Whether administrative rules or Acts of Congress, when a lawsuit arises concerning these enactments, it goes before a judge. Judges interpret or *construe* statutes and regulations, and this results in more case law (judge-made law). So the Common Law is very much alive and well in America.

Legal Training

If the training of "judges" in justice courts is a national embarrassment (discussed in Chapter 5), we can nevertheless be proud of the training that goes on in the nation's 200 accredited law schools.

Law schools teach you to *think like a lawyer*. Unlike other graduate schools, the aim is not to cram a huge body of knowledge into your head so that you may call upon it later. If you get a PhD in, say, Elizabethan Literature, you probably know a lot about the subject and can speak for hours on Shakespeare or Marlowe. But other than brimming with knowledge of the literature of this era, you probably think the same way you did before you began your studies. The study of law is different. In American law schools, students do not read broad summaries of legal principles and then sit through lectures on those principles. The aim is to give you a new way of looking at the world, and actually to think differently about things. You show up on your first day of law school with, as the immortal Professor Kingsley found in *The Paper Chase*, "a head full of mush." What makes law school different from other educational experiences is the method of teaching. The Socratic Method was introduced to American legal training by professor Christopher Columbus Langdell at Harvard Law School in the late nineteenth century. Also known as the casebook method, this way of teaching replaced the rote learning of the substance of law with a give and take between teacher and student, much as Socrates did with his followers. The students are assigned to read a certain number of cases for the next class. In reading the cases, students are told to look for three major areas: the facts, the legal issue, and the holding or decision of the court. If you don't read the cases, you may as well not show up for the class. But that isn't a good strategy because, as in elementary school, attendance is taken. The professor, acting as devil's advocate, poses a question in the form of a *hypothetical*, and then calls on a student to respond and explain why. The professor peppers the student with questions such as:

- "Why should that make a difference?"

- "Why is that important?"

- "I don't see the relevance, explain;"

- "But doesn't your answer conflict with the case that we just discussed?"

- "What if we changed this or that fact – would that change your answer?"

- "Why?"

- "But how can you say X, when you just argued Y?"

This tense interchange is no time for other students to doze off. Right in the middle of questioning Mr. Smith, the professor may turn to Ms. Jones and say: "Mr. Smith said X; do you agree?" "Why?"

Law students discover early on never to ask the meaning of a legal term lest they receive a very cold stare from the professor. If you don't know the meaning of a term, that's what Black's Law Dictionary is for. The students are encouraged to form study groups so that the Socratic dialogue can continue between classes, and the process of learning to "think like a lawyer" never stops.

And so it goes, for 3 or 4 years. When I am asked by a young person about to enter law school if I have any advice, I always say the same thing: "Spin grindstone; apply nose." Review books and summaries are helpful in preparing for exams, but they are not a shortcut to learning the law. They are only useful tools to help you review what you already learned.

Law Review, Moot Court, and Clinical Practice Programs.

Classroom training and late night cramming are not the only ways law students learn the law. The extracurricular programs in American law schools are a key part of the training available.

Law Review is a periodical publication consisting of scholarly articles by law professors, students, and others whose submissions are accepted. To serve on the law review is the pinnacle of achievement for any law student, and it is quite competitive to land a spot as one of the editors. Reviewing, critiquing, and editing complex articles is the most challenging activity a law student can face. Because the law review is published for use by the legal public, the editorial standards are among the highest in any academic profession. Law review articles can have a major influence on the law itself, and are even cited in United States Supreme Court opinions.

Moot Court, as the name implies, is a courtroom activity that doesn't have a real legal outcome, because the result is *moot*. It does, however, provide valuable training for would-be lawyers for a future of arguing cases before judges. The typical moot court program is for appellate arguments, where the law student practices making legal arguments on their feet to a body serving as an appellate court. There are also trial practice courses where students learn the basics of introducing evidence, making objections, and cross-examining witnesses. Just as in college debate societies, there are national moot court competitions, where students from different law schools compete before real judges. Winning a moot court competition is a great resume enhancer, because it shows prospective employers that you know how to put a case together.

Clinical programs. Almost all law schools have programs where the student, under close supervision of a faculty member, actually counsels real clients, typically the poor. The programs can be for landlord-tenant disputes, public benefits applications, or even veterans' affairs. The student gains the valuable experience of dealing with real-life legal problems involving actual clients. The clients gain the benefit of free legal advice.

Every semester there are final exams, and at the end of the whole process is a nasty beast called The Bar Exam that wants to eat your diploma. To prepare for the exam you take a review course, also known as a "cram course." These courses are intensive summaries of everything you have studied over 3 or 4 years. After you pass the bar exam, if you ever do, you then apply to be admitted to the bar, which usually includes a lengthy application form with serious disclosure requirements, as well as an actual in-person interview with a lawyer designated by the authority of the state courts. When you get your license to practice, you start to see the difference your studies have meant to your thinking. The basic skills you acquire in law school are the ability to sort through a complex body of facts, spot the relevant issues, and filter your thoughts into an appropriate area of the law. You learn that to find the answer, you must first ask the right question. You lack the practical knowledge, but that's OK. Any good bar association has primer courses for newly admitted attorneys, and you can always find a fellow lawyer to help you out. If you're in a medium to large law firm, help is always down the hall. There is also Continuing Legal Education (CLE), which is mandatory in most states. CLE consists of courses and seminars conducted by private organizations or by local and state bar associations.

But what about the training of a new judge? Some believe that graduating from law school and a few years of practice is enough, and are comfortable with the idea of a lawyer putting on a robe and ascending the bench right after the swearing in ceremony. The simple reality is that most lawyers have *not* had experience in all of the areas of the law that a judge encounters, with the exception of specialized courts such as bankruptcy, patents, or admiralty. The states vary in their requirements for training newly minted judges, but most have an orientation course or send the new judge to a school called The National Judicial College in Reno, Nevada. This not-for-profit organization, which began in 1963, offers a full curriculum of courses for the judiciary. Its website has a catchy name: www.judges.org. Beyond formal training courses, new judges often rely on their colleagues on the bench for guidance. A new judge can also receive a lot of training from the lawyers before him by ordering briefs on specific areas of the law.

Legal Briefs and Memoranda of Law

A *legal brief* is a document that sets forth the current law involving a case being worked on. A brief is an "argumentative" document. Its purpose is to persuade the reader, and the brief writer is expected to vigorously argue his points and show why the law is on his side. Briefs are typically not brief, and can be book-length. Briefs are different from a *memorandum of law*, which is a document that, like a brief, sets for the law on a case, but it is not argumentative and doesn't urge a point of view. A memorandum of law is typically prepared by an associate in a law firm for a partner, and may include such non-argumentative phrases like: "The law is totally against us on this part of the case." That sentence would not appear in a brief. Notice that a judge "orders" briefs on a subject. He or she does not say: "I don't know what the hell you're talking about, so could you please provide me with summaries of your arguments." No, he simply orders briefs.

Any system operates within an environment that may at times be inhospitable to the system itself. In a nation engulfed in civil strife, all systems suffer, including the legal system. In the next chapter we look at the legal environment of today's America.

CHAPTER 4

The Legal Environment in the Twenty-First Century

I have a statuette on my desk, a gift from my wife Lynda after I graduated from law school. It is a stuffy English barrister, powdered wig and all, holding a book entitled "Law." Inscribed across the base of the statue are the words, "SUE THE BASTARDS." That small statue sums up the legal environment of America today. We are a nation addicted to asserting individual rights.

There were 1,180,386 lawyers in the United States at the end of 2008, an increase of almost ten percent since 2000.[20] According to the United States Census Bureau, the US population grew from 281,481,906 to about 304,500,000 in the same time period, or 9 percent. The percentage of lawyers is outstripping the growth of the population, and for good reason: There's plenty of legal work to go around.

There has been an explosion of laws, rules, regulations, and naturally, lawsuits, and that explosion affects every aspect of American life, from our everyday business activities to the nation's economy. A new survey commissioned by the advocacy organization Common Good and conducted by Harris Interactive, found that only 16 percent of the American adults surveyed trust the legal system to defend them against baseless claims. Fifty-four percent do not trust the legal system, and 30 percent are not sure. An amazing 76 percent of those surveyed agree that fear of frivolous lawsuits discourages people from performing normal activities.[21] There was a time, not long ago, when we thought of a courtroom as a place where you go to solve a dispute. You accused someone, or someone accused you, of breaching a contract, of committing a tort against you, of destroying your property, or some other wrong. Corporations would slug it out over contract disputes, intellectual property issues, or antitrust matters. Someone or something "did you wrong" and to correct the wrong you sought "your day in court." If a matter was small and couldn't support the hiring of a lawyer, you had small claims court. Many disputes were handled over a kitchen table, in a boardroom, a diner, or on a golf course. You ironed it out. Big cases were complicated and you needed to hire a lawyer. Your legal dispute was based on caselaw, a statute, or a regulation. The automatic thinking, at least among individuals, was that you would find a way to handle it. Priests, ministers, rabbis, friends, and neighbors were often the people you would consult. If there was a local government issue, such as a pothole in front of your house, you would go to your local committeeman or alderman, who would make a couple of phone calls. You did not think of the courtroom as a way of eliminating all of the vexations of life, but as a court of last resort. There arose in the second half of the twentieth century a phenomenon: the courtroom as the court of *first* resort. Part of the problem is that the costs of hiring a lawyer is sometimes zero, so why not sue. If you have no money at stake, what is there to lose? Personal injury cases are handled on a contingent fee basis, which means no monetary outlay by the plaintiff. You see the ads: "Free consultation with no risk to you." For any of a variety of perceived constitutional wrongs, the American Civil Liberties Union, or various other issue orientated organizations will step up to the plate for you.

What constitutes a *wrong* has gone through a transformation, not just in the law, but in our heads. There is the infamous and familiar case of 6-year-old Zachary Christie of Delaware. In October 2009, he received a 45-day suspension from school for bringing to school his new Cub Scout camping utensil – a combined spoon, fork, and knife – to eat his lunch. Only after national media attention and public outrage did the school district decide to reinstate Zachary and remove the suspension from his record. Stories like this have prompted many state legislatures, including Colorado, Florida, Indiana, Rhode Island, and Texas to revise their school discipline laws. This insanity can't be blamed on lawyers, and certainly not judges. It is a societal problem wherein there appears to be a new social contract emerging that disposes us to seek redress at law for the vicissitudes of life. The Zachary Christie fiasco was the result of a legal beastie called *zero tolerance* policy on weapons in school. Zero tolerance no doubt arose out of a legitimate concern about weapons in schools. Children and others are injured and killed by deadly weapons and they have no place whatsoever in a school. While it sounds like a good idea at first blush, zero tolerance really means that local officials, principals, administrators, or teachers, simply give up on intelligent discretion and hide behind the zero tolerance policy, out of fear of being sued. Zero tolerance means zero discretion, zero thinking, and zero decision-making. It results in adults acting like idiots. The mindset seems to be that absolute compliance never got anyone in trouble.

What did Sister Mary Agnes know that we have forgotten?

I recall Sister Mary Agnes of my elementary school years in the 1950s. We all thought of her as a figurative as well as a literal big sister. She loved kids. If a student was caught out of line, she would put him in a headlock and deliver gentle knocks to his skull with her knuckles, all the while stifling a laugh. She laughed because she was not concerned about seeing a process server a few days later armed with a document accusing her of assault, battery, endangering the welfare of a child, or other nefarious deeds. She thought she was merely bopping knuckles to a brat's head; she did not perceive it as a *wrong*. Today's schoolyard is a bramble bush of wrongs waiting to happen. No safety surfacing under the jungle gym? Call the school attorney. Dodgeball during recess? Please. First it encourages aggressive behavior, possibly launching a child on a life of violence. Secondly, it risks abrasions, a wrong if there ever was one. Billy pulled Peggy's pigtail? Call the Crisis Intervention Hotline, after making careful note of the time and collecting the names of witnesses. Jot down a memorandum noting exactly where you were at the time of Billy's act, and what steps you took (or could have taken – but don't write this down) to avoid the incident. Consider a Grief Counselor for Peggy. To be sure, there are serious problems that occur in schools. Physical and sexual abuse does exist and must be addressed, and legal artillery should be called in on these incidents, not on events where children are simply behaving like children.

In days gone by, if your committee wanted to have fireworks at your church's Fourth of July picnic, you only thought about the cost of the fireworks. Today you need to consult the local fire department, village, town, and possibly the county; forget about it anyway because your state probably forbids fireworks unless you have a special license. If you wanted to pave your parking lot, you would call the paving guy. Now you need an engineer to prepare a site plan with details about lighting and the exact types of planting you need to put around the perimeter and of course paying heed to the exact number of handicapped parking spaces that are required. In the past, if you wanted to start a business you would, well, start a business. Now you must inquire of the various levels of government about the need for a Certificate of Authority, a tax ID, and, depending on what you are going to do, see if you need a license, special schooling, and, perhaps, a waiting period. Slip up, and you have committed a wrong; you may wind up in court.

This is the new legal environment that judges, lawyers, and litigants labor in. A trial judge would much prefer to attend to the serious felonies and major civil cases on her docket than waste judicial and societal time adjudicating dodge ball incidents. But the one thing a judge does not get to do is to pick the kind of cases that she wants to deal with.

The Entitlement State

The Progressive Era that began in the 1880s launched some badly needed reforms, including prohibitions on child labor, breaking up monopolistic trusts, correcting labor injustices, and not to mention, women's suffrage. Political bosses and financial oligarchs used to create the reality of life, and the average citizen was left to the whims of *The Man*. But another dynamic of the progressive movement, one based on good intentions, was the notion that the government should take care of people and protect them from the problems of life. Government came to be seen, not just as an apparatus of enforcing objective laws, but as a machine for setting right all of the wrongs of life. What has happened in the nation, especially since the 1960s, has been a vast expansion of what is considered a right. The Constitution was written as a document that basically said what government couldn't do. It is now thought of as a font of individual rights that beg to be asserted. We cherish our civil rights and our property rights, but just what you have a right to has now come to be thought of as a piece of property.

Thus began the growth of the entitlement state, a state where the government would provide you with goods and services that you might have to do without if left to the uncertainties of living. This philosophy of government saw its real flowering during Franklin Roosevelt's New Deal in the 1930s. The idea that competition and free markets would provide for the greater good crashed head-on with the Great Depression. The belief took hold that capitalism somehow had failed. Books are still being written disputing that notion, and there are cogent arguments that the New Deal programs such as the Works Progress Administration and the alphabet soup of other federal programs actually exacerbated the depression. Unemployment was about the same in 1939 as it was in 1930. But the historical truth has been written: we are a nation increasingly in love with our government-provided goods and services, our entitlements.

The problem with entitlements is contained in the very word itself, the idea that we are *entitled* to this or that governmental benefit, not that the benefits seem like a nice idea, but that – "It's mine; fork it over." The benefit has become a *right*. If you think otherwise, look to the headlines from Europe about violent riots against any government move to reduce state spending by scaling back on the sacred entitlements. In France 20-somethings torched cars and smashed windows because of the horrible specter of having to wait until they are 62 to retire, rather than 60. Poor dears. In Greece, where cheating on taxes is a national pastime, similar riots occurred over government moves to reduce benefits. Here in America we see students demonstrating against any increase tuition increase at state-run universities. As the nation still struggles from the aftermath of the Great Recession, discussions of public employee union give-backs or even future trimming is met with stanch resistance. Teachers unions rail against any discussion of lay-offs, but adamantly refuse to take a pay cut or even agree to a lower annual pension increase. "Don't lay off my colleagues, but if keeping them on the payroll means reducing my benefits, by all means do so." This is the real problem with entitlements: they corrupt civic virtue, that commonly understood concept of shared responsibility and shared sacrifice. Civic virtue asks us to look beyond our parochial interests from time to time, and consider the wider good. Entitlements change us as people, away from the notion of the common good, to a people who want theirs, the common good be damned. Entitlements infantilize us. Try negotiating with a 5-year-old. The kid is hungry and wants to eat, NOW. You try to explain that the next rest stop is 50 miles away, and you will pull off then for lunch. Good luck. Now means *now*, and don't talk to me about this reality stuff. Compare this to a public employee union that wants both a raise and pension benefit increase in this contract, now, even though the revenues to pay for the raises have been slashed because of economic conditions. It is now an open secret that lavish publicly funded pensions are based on ridiculous actuarial assumptions made years ago by politicians who are no longer in office. As New Jersey Governor Chris Christie so aptly put it: "The chickens have come home to roost." But don't talk about economic hard times and the inescapable reality that the fiscal status quo is impossible. Now means now. Only recently has it become possible for a politician to actually suggest that our economic future demands that we trim entitlement spending to conform to reality. The problem has always been, and still continues, that once an entitlement becomes a fact, people are loathe to let go. That's why they are called entitlements.

Entitlements are good for lawyers. When a benefit becomes an entitlement through law, withholding that entitlement means a violation of law, and the job of correcting that problem falls to lawyers – and bureaucrats. Everybody loves to blame lawyers, but the blame is misplaced.[22] If a client walks into a lawyer's office and presents a set of facts that the lawyer determines to be a violation of, say, the Fair Labor Standards Act, it is the lawyer's job to seek to seek justice for the client. It's not just her job, it's her sworn responsibility. It is not the lawyer's job to say to the client that this particular entitlement is crazy and that it destroys jobs and will damage the economy. No. It is the lawyer's job to act on behalf of her client.

Can Empowerment mean less Power?

It has become an article of faith, especially among liberals, that our newfound "rights" empower us as individuals. There was a time when a school principal, faced with a disciplinary problem, would simply make a decision. Decision-making in the public sphere has become almost an old joke. In place of individual power to make decisions, we now see layers and layers of regulations, fashioned by well-intentioned regulation writers. If something doesn't work, make a rule. If that doesn't work, write a few more rules.

No school administrator wants his school to be placed on a list of dangerous institutions. At Jamaica High School in Queens, New York, an assistant principal noticed that assistant deans were calling 911 in response to violent situations. One of the results was that the school was placed on a city list of dangerous schools. Problem? Make a rule. He sent out a one sentence instruction that said: "Deans are not permitted to call 911 *for any reason*." The rule was as simple in its clarity (a good characteristic of any rule) as it was insane in its removal of sound discretion. Mariya Fatima, a ninth-grade student, suffered a stroke. Because of the memo, employees waited over 1 hour before calling for emergency medical aid, a delay that has made her paralysis worse.[23] Rule-making strips power away from individuals who really need the power, the discretion to make on-the-spot decisions.

Anyone who has ever encountered a local building department has seen up-close how rules, as opposed to intelligent discretion, can result in a nightmare. I have a friend who runs a municipal golf course. He wanted to put a canvas cover over the tee-off spots on the driving range so that golfers could use the driving range in the rain. Great idea – more money for both him and the municipality. Not so fast. There was a building department rule that required that all new structures be able

67

to withstand a wind of 120 MPH. He tried to explain that the "structure" was simply going to be a pipe frame with canvas on the top. If he forgot to roll up the canvas before a hurricane, so what? What damage could a piece of flying canvas do? But no. A structure is a structure, and the new building code says it must be able to handle a hurricane. In a sane world, the building inspector could have made a decision that his proposal was not contemplated by the rule, or at most the inspector would have passed it by his supervisor for a written ruling. But the inspector was not in charge: the building code was. It is easy to argue, as bureaucrats do, that rules and regulations make for a just and predictable world. We are, after all, a nation of law, not men. But no set of regulations or laws can possibly cover every contingency, and to remove the ability of people to make flexible interpretations actually robs everyone of power.

When I was Chairman of the Long Island Maritime Museum, a subject came up at almost every board meeting: weeds were infiltrating our small craft exhibit building. The Museum is located on property owned by the County of Suffolk, and anything that went on at the museum was covered by county regulations. The building was once an airplane hanger, with a beautiful old classic design, and it was one of the most important structures on the museum site. The weed problem could not be simply solved by periodic "weed-wacking," because the weeds would infiltrate at the base of the metal structure, along with the moisture that weeds carry with them. Rust was beginning to endanger the foundation. So I had a simple solution, which caused a government member of our board to have an apoplectic fit. I suggested that we simp_y spray the perimeter with the popular weed control chemical Roundup®.

The building, as fate would have it, was located about 50 yards from the Great South Bay. County, state, and, presumable United Nations rules forbade the use of any chemical defoliants within a certain distance to any body of water, a distance greater than that of our building. Now you are probably familiar with Roundup. You spray it on the offending vegetation, and within a few days the stuff is dead, and so is the Roundup. It becomes an inert chemical within days. The substance would be no more likely to seep into the bay than it would be to infect the moon. No matter! A rule is a rule, a reg is a reg, and no commissioner is empowered to make exceptions. One day the building is going to collapse, along with the beautiful restored vessels it contains – for no sane reason.

Flexible decision-making works for humanity – better than robotic rule-following. After the 1994 earthquake in Los Angeles knocked down a number of freeways across the city, California Governor Pete Wilson was faced with a choice. Stand by and watch the building code and the multitude of other regulations work their wonder for a few years, or do his job for the people who elected him. He decided to fast-track the repairs, recognizing the obvious fact that the people of LA needed the freeways – fast. He ditched the rule books, and with the help of federal disaster aid, provided for financial incentives to get contractors to do the job pronto. The freeways went back up within 66 days – not years. Leadership, allowed to happen. He could have let the regulatory process take over, and as LA coped without freeways for a few years, he could have hid behind the traditional cover of the bureaucracy: "I don't write the rules; I just enforce them."

Justice would be far better served if we empowered people in positions of authority to exercise that authority.

Due Process for Everybody

The Fifth Amendment of the United States Constitution states that: "No person shall be…deprived of life, liberty or property without due process of law." This is one of the foundation blocks of our republic that makes it the great nation it is. If a cop pounds on your door, there are procedures that he has to follow – due process – and those procedures protect our freedom. The idea behind due process was to keep you from being thrown in jail arbitrarily, or to keep your property from being confiscated without a lot of safeguards. But in modern America, we have a gut belief that we are entitled to due process in a wild array of situations, especially schools, because public school enrollment has been determined to be a property right. If a principal wants to send a kid home for misbehavior, hold the phone! The kid is entitled to due process, which usually means hearings, reports, and meetings. If the same principal wants to fire a teacher for whatever reason, he had best consult the foot thick union contract that provides for a bewildering list of due process requirements. If a teacher knocks off 10 points on a student's grade because an assignment was handed in late, she had best be prepared for a fight, because some parent no doubt believes that due process requires much more than red pen strokes on paper.

Rights used to be understood to be those things that *government* could not take from us – without due process. Rights are now understood to be autonomous things that we use to bash each other.

This is the legal environment of the United States in the early 21st Century. Justice in America is going through some revolutionary times, and societal norms as well as economics have an impact as never before. In the next chapter we meet the people who are at the forefront of dispensing justice in America, our judges.

CHAPTER 5

Judges – The People
Who Administer the System

They wear classic black robes. When they enter a courtroom we are ordered to stand, pay attention, and set aside all other business. Some courts, especially the United States Supreme Court, but many lower courts as well, still use the quaint, and intimidating, way of introducing the judge: "Oyez! Oyez! Oyez! All persons having business before this Honorable, Court are admonished to draw near and give their attention, for the Court is now in session. God save the United States and this Honorable Court!" Gulp! You have no doubt that something important is about to happen. Put down that newspaper, take the gum out of your mouth, and holster your Blackberry. You are in a special place.

We call judges "Your Honor" and we approach their "bench" only when called. They don't report to a boss in a typical employer-employee sense. They control their own workload and decide when it's time to go home, or to golf. They don't have to explain their decisions, especially to the press. Some are appointed or elected to very long terms; some are appointed for life. Some have modest pensions; some can retire at full pay after 15 years. Some carry heavy caseloads, give speeches, teach classes, and write books. They are former lawyers, for the most part, but not always. They are mean-spirited creeps; they are humane and caring folks; they are brilliant and hard working; they are dumb-as-a-rock and lazy; they are sometimes all of these things in a single day. Some may suffer from "Judge's disease," the symptoms of which include "pomposity, irritability, talkativeness, proneness to *obiter dicta* (statements not necessary to the outcome of a case), and a tendency to take shortcuts."[24] Some lose their marbles. Judges are like all of us; difference is, they are very powerful.

Qualifications to Become a Judge

Alexander Hamilton, one of the framers of the United States Constitution, writing about the qualifications of judges, said it well: "There can be but few men in the society who will have sufficient skill in the laws to qualify them for the stations of judges. And making the proper deductions for the ordinary depravity of human nature, the number must be still smaller of those who unite the requisite integrity with the requisite knowledge."[25] Judge Bernard Sheintag, a New York Appellate Court judge in the 1940s and 1950s, identified eight virtues that a judge should possess: independence, courtesy and patience, dignity (but not excluding humor), open mindedness, impartiality, thoroughness and decisiveness, an understanding heart and social consciousness.[26] It isn't a job for everyone; few meet the necessary qualifications, although there is great controversy over what those qualifications are and who gets to decide them. A judge in the American system, whether appointed or elected, goes through a selection process that usually sorts out those who are unfit for the job. But the sorting process is not foolproof: occasionally mistakes are made, and sometimes an incompetent idiot gets to put on a black robe – and sometimes an innocent person gets sentenced to death.

A judge must be impartial, and should rule regardless of his personal biases. That is not controversial – who could argue otherwise? Everyone would agree that a judge should make a decision based on the law and not based on a preconceived notion of what the outcome should be or on his personal opinion of the character of the defendant. But that is as easy as saying "food should taste good." Sometimes it tastes bad, sometimes it makes you sick, and occasionally it can kill you. We can all understand outright bias, and why it cannot be tolerated in a judge. Who could argue that a judge should recuse himself (remove himself from the case) if he is deciding a case where he holds a major financial stake in a corporation that is one of the parties? Who can deny that a judge should not sit on a case where one of the litigants is his immediate family member? What about a case where one of the parties was a key contributor to his last campaign for office, or to his opponent? A major Supreme Court case addressed that issue exactly and is discussed in Chapter Six. For a judge to refuse to hear a case where he has an obvious bias is expected. As Supreme Court Justice Felix Frankfurter once observed, there are three qualities that a judge needs to have, all of which are *disinterestedness*.[27] Chief Justice John Roberts famously said in his Senate confirmation hearings that the job of a judge is akin to that of an umpire, calling balls and strikes. But what about bias that is beneath the surface of thought, bias that the judge may not even be aware of – subconscious bias – all of those little things in life that have happened to us and make us who we are. You have a gut negativity toward police officers because as a child you saw your beloved uncle whacked over the head with a nightstick. You don't consciously recall the incident, but it is there in your subconscious forever. The field of neuroscience is forever uncovering those hidden and forgotten thoughts that shoot through our brains like the flash of a light, and of which we are totally unaware. Because "Judges are men, not disembodied spirits," they, like all of us, carry with them the whole bundle of prejudices that have formed their lives.[28] Supreme Court Justice Benjamin Cardozo stated this truth eloquently:" The great tides of and currents which engulf the rest of men do not turn aside in their course and pass the judges by..."[29] If one defines bias, impartiality or disinterestedness with a "total absence of preconceptions in the mind of the judge, then no one has ever had a fair trial and no one ever will."[30]

Is Chief Justice Robert's "umpire" analogy correct? Does it explain the job of a judge and how a judge thinks, or is it an oversimplification? After all, what is a ball and what is a strike? Is it how the umpire sees it or is it an objective application of the rules of baseball? Legal scholar and Seventh Circuit Court Judge Richard Posner questions Justice Robert's analogy. "Against Robert's umpireal analogy, therefore, I set the story of three umpires asked to explain the epistemology of balls and strikes. The first umpire explains that he calls them as they are, the second that he calls them as he sees them, and the third that there are no balls and strikes until he calls them. The first umpire is the *legalist*. The second is the *pragmatic* trial judge (as he sees them). The third is the appellate judge deciding cases in the *open area* [that is, cases that cannot be decided by a simple application of a legal rule to a set of facts]. His activity is creation rather than discovery."[31] (Emphases added). It is often said, ad nauseam, in Senate Confirmation Hearings, that judges should not "legislate from the bench." But the real question is not whether judges do or should legislate from the bench, but whether it is even possible not to in certain cases. In a republican democracy it's in our blood to think that elected legislators actually write the laws, and that judges are left only to interpret them. The thinking is that in a deliberative body like a legislature, all sides get to speak and all views are aired, and the voters are heard through their elected representatives. But consider the historic Health Care Bill of 2010, voted on by the House of Representatives on Sunday, March 21, 2010. The House, the press, the public, the President of the United States, and late night comedy writers had 2 days to read, consider, and comment on a 2,000 page bill – 12 times the size of the United States Constitution. Was this enough time to deliberate on a document, the goal of which was to change the health care system in the United States? The British satirist A. P. Herbert ascribed these words to one of his characters, the Lord Chancellor, exclaiming "The pity is that there is not more judge-made law. For most of His Majesty's judges are much better fitted for the making of laws than the queer and cowardly rabble who are elected to Parliament for that purpose by the fantastic machinery of universal suffrage."[32] Herbert has been attacked over the years in various publications by those who don't realize that the cases he writes about are fiction. Before you accuse him of antidemocratic bias, I remind you that Herbert was a satirist.

How Judges get their Jobs

With a bang of the gavel a judge can sentence you to death or hard labor, stop a gigantic construction project, or reverse an executive order of the President of the United States. A judge can award custody of children, divvy up marital property, or set aside a verdict of 12 jurors. He can change the course of American business (Remember what we used to call "The Telephone Company"?) or alter the shape of school districts across an entire state. He can put a lawyer in jail for contempt (no wonder more people don't want to be judges) or order a convicted killer to be set free.

Who are these people? How do they get to their positions of power? Are they smarter than average? Do they all come from top tier schools and did they get excellent grades? Are they politically ambitious or just dedicated to public service? Do they have a temperament superior to that of lesser souls? Are they possessed of a certain wisdom that the rest of us lack? How in the world did they get there? Is he a seasoned legislator or public executive with vast experience in legal matters? Is he a political hack enjoying the twilight of his working years, appointed by some old friends as a reward for screwing up his legislative career? Is she a talented schmoozer who knows how to work the floor at bar association meetings, getting to know the lawyers on the selection commission? Is she a brilliant intellect, well known for her talents in the courtroom as well as her scholarly writings in various publications? Is he a gifted retail politician who knows how to ring doorbells, press the flesh, and get out the vote? Is she the Governor's sister-in-law?

America is unique in that we the people elect judges in many of our states. It is a changing landscape, with many states opting for "merit" selection, picking candidates based on their qualifications. Many question whether "merit selection" is an untainted good idea, or just an idea with a good title. You may be surprised.

Chapter Six addresses the various ways judges are selected across the country (political, merit, nominating commissions, executive appointments, etc.). The majority of states provide for popular election of judges on at least one level. The American way of selecting judges drive European pundits absolutely insane, especially the French (of course). Europeans see the bench as a career to be prepared for, not won in an election. A judicial career in most of the world is considered just that – a career, and one prepares for it as one would prepare for a career in science, engineering, or medicine. The growing trend toward "merit selection" of judges is taking hold in the United States. It's hard to argue that a judge should be chosen for something other than merit. But as we shall see in Chapter Six, appointing judges does not guarantee quality and electing judges does not lower quality. The issue always on the table is politics, and how to take it out of the judicial selection system. I will discuss how the appointment process, such as merit selection, has as much risk of political influence as contested elections, perhaps more. Also in Chapter Six the problem of money and its possible corrupting effects is also reviewed, including the *Caperton* case, a major Supreme Court decision on how political contributions can influence the judicial process. If you enjoy reading stinging dissents, you will love the words of Chief Justice Roberts and Justice Scalia on the mischief this case may cause.

There is a great ongoing smackdown between conservatives and liberals in our country about "legislating from the bench," and strict versus loose construction (of the words of the Constitution). The conservatives hone to the principle of Original Intent of the Framers of the Constitution, and of giving deference to the will of the legislature (even though most legislators don't read the stuff they vote on). Liberals desire to "do the right thing" no matter what the legislature thinks. Both sides accuse the other of being "activist," which, if taken from the context of the writings, may be defined as : "You are on the wrong side."

An American judge holds a unique position of in society. On matters large and small, we place decisions in the hands of one person, and expect that person to get it right. What makes a judge try to "get it right"? This goes to the subject of motivations and constraints, both positive and negative, on what a judge does. Suppose Judge Smith comes to the bench at the age of 51, has a 14-year appointment, and a generous pension. She might think: "If I don't make waves and keep my head low, I'll retire at 65 so why try too hard?" This question gets to the core of judicial character and behavior. Because many of the normal employer-employee constraints don't exist for a judge, the impetus to do a good job has to come from somewhere else. In a typical employer-employee relationship, even a managerial one, the employee knows that he can be fired, transferred, suffer a pay reduction, or otherwise have a career malfunction if he does not do a good job. This is so whether the organization is for-profit or not. These things result in constraints on an employee's behavior: if your actions or inactions result in a bullseye on your butt, don't be surprised by the occasional sting of an arrow. There are no bullseyes on judges' butts. Their behavior is shaped by other constraints. Here are a few of the behavior inducing constraints on judges.

1. The desire to do a good job. A lot of people are motivated by this alone.

2. Avoiding reversal on appeal. It can be embarrassing, and if frequent, will be picked up by the press.

3. The desire to look good in front of one's peers. While having lunch with other judges, one doesn't want to be known as the slob whose docket (list of active cases) is two years behind everyone else's.

4. The Chief Administrative Judge is watching. While she can't overrule you, she can make life unpleasant by assigning unpleasant chores, such as Arraignment Calendar on Christmas Day.

If a judge doesn't think this is his last job, a poor record on the bench does not make for a spiffy resume, especially if he is seeking political office ("He couldn't control his own courtroom – How do you expect him to run the Great State of ..."). The constraints and motivations of the job are discussed in Chapter Nine.

Judicial Pay

Judicial pay is an ongoing controversy, certainly among judges, but also among any concerned citizen who wants to see institutions function properly. John Roberts, Chief Justice of the United States Supreme Court, is head of the federal courts, and honorary leader of the entire American judiciary. He is a proponent of the idea that judicial pay is too low. The late Justice Rehnquist, his predecessor, was also of this opinion. Justice Roberts' thinking is that substantial salaries are needed to attract talented people, a belief as American as a Norman

Rockwell painting. This is why Goldman Sachs, AIG et. al. pay $100 million bonuses to their star producers lest they defect to, what, professional wrestling? By any objective measure, judges are not paid enough, especially in view of the enormous responsibilities they shoulder. There are objective studies, as we shall see, showing how the modesty of judicial pay is causing seasoned judges to retire early, leaving an experience gap. But let's slow down and take a careful look at the issue of adequate compensation. I will discuss some reasons why judicial pay should be higher, certainly better than it is now, but not extremely high. We don't want to attract lawyers who are really motivated to escape the stress of a high-paid law practice and replace it with a high-paid spot on the bench. We don't want a judicial career to be perceived as somewhere to go to relax. The issue of judicial compensation is addressed in Chapter Seven.

Educating Judges

Judicial training is a serious matter, but not one that is taken too seriously. Consider a newly elected or appointed judge. He has had a reasonably distinguished career as a lawyer but was limited to representing insurance companies in personal injury cases. As a new judge of general jurisdiction, he will be faced with a panoply of cases, including criminal, matrimonial, commercial litigation, and perhaps intellectual property disputes, all of which he knows absolutely nothing about beyond what he studied in law school many years ago. Yes, he did graduate from law school, did well, and has successfully practiced law for years, but he needs to review the substantive law of many fields to be effective.

He takes the bench and his first case is a serious contested divorce; he knows nothing about matrimonial law,
except that he is happily married. There are schools
where newly hatched judges can go to get up to speed
but the system is far from uniform throughout the country. It is just plain dumb for a new judge not to go to a
refresher school. There is every reason for a new judge
to enroll in formal training.

Should Judges be Lawyers? The Justice of the Peace Debate

If Frank Capra made a movie about judges he would
have chosen the Justice of the Peace court system as
his dramatic, if not comedic, setting. A Justice of the
Peace, an official who typically has no formal legal training, is an anachronism in the American legal system.
Often called Justice Courts, in many states the position
has been replaced by a *magistrate*, who may or may not
have legal training. The office harkens back to a time
when there were few trained lawyers to go around, and
the local government needed to appoint someone to this
position to hear minor cases. They often hear traffic
cases, misdemeanors, and various small claims matters,
with a limit in the amount at suit, usually no more than
$10,000. They also perform marriages. If you Google
"justice of the peace," the first three paid listings that
appear are offers to perform civil marriages, although
the links are not to actual justices of the peace. Many
of these charming local courts do not have court ste-
nographers or even recording devices, and many judges
do not even take notes. Without a record, appeals are
impossible. There is often no way of knowing what has

transpired. The courtroom may be a converted garage, a library reading room, or the judge's kitchen. Even today some insist that having a non-lawyer judge is good for the system because it brings a "fresh perspective." "Why should we exclude from the bench," the argument goes, "people of fine character, good intelligence, public spiritedness, and keen judgment just because they didn't graduate from law school and pass a bar exam?" That, indeed is the basic argument for justice courts, and the stupidity of it cannot be overstated. The same argument could be made for appointing a medical director of a municipal hospital without a medical degree. Any person who possesses those fine characteristics and wants to be a judge at any level should go to law school and pass the bar exam. There is no reason why a person who occupies such a key position in our system of law should not be formally trained in the law. We would not want a poet as a city engineer or a cab driver as Municipal Plumbing Inspector. A person whose job is to dispense law should be trained in, well, the law.

There are over 6,000 Justices of the Peace and Magistrate Judges in the country.[33] States with Justices of the Peace include Arizona, Delaware, Louisiana, Mississippi, Montana, Nevada, New York, Oregon, Texas, and Utah. States with Magistrate judges are Alaska, Delaware (note – both) Georgia, Idaho, Iowa, Kansas, North Carolina, Oregon, Rhode Island, South Carolina, Vermont, West Virginia, and Wyoming.

Some states are gradually abandoning these positions or are replacing them with licensed lawyers. California, for example, began replacing justices of the peace with licensed attorneys in 1974, after a unanimous California Supreme Court held that it was a violation of the federal right to due process under the Fourteenth Amendment to allow a non-lawyer justice to preside over a case that could result in jail time.[34] In New York, an organization known as New York State Magistrates Association, vehemently opposes bills in both the senate and the assembly that would give a criminal defendant a right to have his case heard before a judge who is an admitted attorney, an "opt-out rule." The memorandum of opposition, which is posted on the association's website (http://nysmagassoc.homestead.com) notes that 67% of New York's 1,500 or so town and village justices are not attorneys, as if this is something to brag about. The memorandum cites (with incomplete citation form that would make a first-week law student shudder) a 1983 case that held that a criminal has no such right. But whether or not it is a legal right for a criminal to have an attorney as a judge, the non-attorney justice of the peace system makes no sense. Ours is no longer an agrarian nation where population centers are sparse and widely dispersed, and transportation onerous. A common argument is that the system would be overloaded if cases had to be heard by judges who are licensed lawyers. But this is an echo of times past when there were few lawyers, which is hardly the situation now. Most of these positions are part time jobs, so finding trained and licensed attorneys to fill the spots is not a challenging task, even if the pay is modest. A call to civic duty is not rare among lawyers. Why do we find lawyers sitting on not-for-profit boards, school boards, and library boards? These positions seldom pay, so even if the compensation for a Justice of the Peace or Magistrate job is modest, there is no reason to believe there won't be plenty of attorney-applicants for open positions. But attempts to change the system have often resulted in firm opposition.

Undereducated and poorly trained judges are not just theoretical problems. The *New York Times* published a three part series in 2006 about the local justice courts in New York State entitled "Broken Bench."[35] The system is replete with incidents of defendants who were jailed without bail or without being advised of the right to an attorney, of judges refusing to grant protective orders, and in one matter, dismissing a case based on a judge's discussion with a local municipal official without the defendant municipality even showing up. A woman from upstate New York, a mother of four, sought an order of protection against her husband, who allegedly choked her, kicked her in the stomach, and threatened to kill her. The justice, a former state trooper with only a high school diploma, not only refused to issue the order, but later told his court clerk, "Every woman needs a good pounding every now and then."[36] A 76-year-old man who contested a speeding ticket was jailed without warning for 3 days in 2003 because he called the sheriff's deputy a liar. One judge, a retired factory worker, turned his courtroom into a collection agency for local business owners. A Louisiana justice of the peace, Justice Keith Bardwell, made worldwide headlines recently when he refused to perform a marriage for a mixed race couple. According to Judge Bardwell, he refuses to marry inter-racial couples because of his concern for the offspring of the marriage, who, he has determined, won't be accepted by either race. Perhaps he is worried that one of the mixed race kids may grow up to be President of the United States. He notes that he has "...piles and piles of black friends" and that when they come to his house they even "use my bathroom." What a guy! He apparently never heard of the case of *Loving v. Virginia,* a 1967 US Supreme Court case that found laws against inter-racial marriages unconstitutional.[37] I called the Louisiana State Bar Association and was not surprised to discover that Judge Bardwell is not an attorney. He resigned his position as justice of the peace in Tangipahoa Parish in November 2009, amidst widespread calls for his ouster, including one from Louisiana Governor Bobby Jindall. But this was a headline making case. Because there are usually no recordings of the proceedings, violations of the law occur every day in these ersatz courtrooms.

Many attorneys try to avoid justice courts because they are frustrated that the "justices" cannot understand their legal arguments. One New York justice of the peace, a phone-company repairman, would curse at defendants and jail them without bail or even a trial, state disciplinary officials found. In a case involving a loose dog, he ordered the dog killed and then he threatened its owner with jail. One of the biggest problems is not that the local judges aren't trained in the law, but that they often have very little formal education of any kind. The *New York Times* noted that in 2006 of the 75% of the judges who are not attorneys, over 400 of them, about one third, do not have any education beyond high school and of those 40 have not even graduated from high school.

If the lack of educational requirements is shocking, the training of non-lawyer justices is worse. Until recently New York only required 1 week of training in the law with a 50-question true-false test at the end. The passing grade was 70. If you fail, you get to retake the exam as needed. In 2006, the New York State Office of Court Administration launched an "Action Plan" to improve the Justice Court system. In the 2-year update report in 2008, we see that the educational requirements have tightened up. The report states that the changes in the training requirements are "...particularly dramatic."[38] The drama we witness is this: classroom time has been extended from 1 week to 2, and 4 weeks of in-home study have been added, and there is a provision for continuing educational seminars. After this "training" these folks are set loose to sit in judgment over their fellow citizens. And the problem shows little sign of improvement in New York. In January 2010, the *New York Times* reported that a bill to make minor changes to the system had stalled in the state legislature.[39] The proposal would have given a criminal defendant the right to have his case heard by a judge who is a lawyer, similar to the "opt out" system in California. The system is so mired in local politics that even a special 31 member commission could not muster the support necessary. A working political compromise should be obvious: simply grandfather the existing non-lawyer judge positions, but change the law to require any future justice of the peace to have graduated from an accredited law school, pass the bar exam, and hold a license to practice law. Add to the bill more stringent continuing education requirements for sitting judges. This seems like a simple way to cure an ongoing national embarrassment, but don't hold your breath. A justice of the peace should be a relic of old time movies, not a part of the American system of law.

In the next chapter we look at the way we select our judges in the United States.

CHAPTER 6

How We Select Our Judges

Popular election of judges is a perfect example of American Exceptionalism. Experts in the field of judicial selection say that only two countries outside of the United States elect judges by popular vote, and then, only in a limited way.[40] In Switzerland, judges are elected in some smaller jurisdictions, and in Japan members of the Supreme Court face possible retention elections. Hans A. Linde, a former justice of the Oregon Supreme Court said at a 1988 symposium on judicial selection, "To the rest of the world American adherence to judicial elections is as incomprehensible as our rejection of the metric system."[41] In France, for example, prospective judges must endure a rigorous battery of exams and then must attend a 2- year course of study beyond law school.

Partisan election of judges appears on the surface to be a simple and proper exercise of democracy. A judge is, after all, a public official, and should be accountable to the electorate through the time-honored way of keeping a politician's feet to the fire – the ballot box. The occasional horrors of judicial misconduct would disappear, the argument goes, if the offending judge were to face an upcoming election. But, as we shall see below, the prospect of facing the voters may taint a judge's impartiality. With an election looming, how likely is it for a judge to dismiss a notorious case against a murder suspect, even though the evidence clearly calls for his release?

A judicial election campaign is different from that of a typical office-seeker. A politician running for town council will tell voters that she intends to hold down taxes, clean up the mess in town hall, make the streets safer, and press whatever other hot-button issues work. A person running for judge, on the other hand, is limited to what he can say. He can't promise to decide cases in a certain way, or to reverse a law that has been enacted. He really can't talk about anything that he might do in the future, and is limited to talking about his background and how it qualifies him for the bench. But how does that resonate with voters? It doesn't, and that is one of the problems with running for judge; it's hard to get voters excited about your campaign, which, in turn, means it's hard to get people to know you.

In America, 87 percent of all state court judges must face elections.[42] There are different paths to the bench, and the path chosen depends on the state and the specific office sought. There are partisan elections, non-partisan elections, retention elections (one gets there by appointment and then must face the voters after a set number of years on the bench) merit selection, direct appointment and various in-between hybrids. The process of selecting judges has been changed and tweaked ever since the founding of the republic and the states vary greatly in how the process moves forward.[43]

The Problem of Money in the Election of Judges

The American Bar Association's Model Code of Judicial Conduct states, in the first canon:

"A judge shall uphold and promote the independence, integrity, and impartiality of the judiciary, and shall avoid impropriety and the appearance of impropriety."[44]

Money and impartiality have always been quarrelsome bedfellows, and the stew of judicial campaign financing has been simmering for years. In the 39 states that have some form of contested elections, the way to judicial office is the same as any elective office: fundraising. A judge running for office is often unknown to the voters, and the only way to get known is to campaign, and that includes advertising, and that requires money – lots of it. Direct contributions to a judicial office-seeker are controlled by various state statutory schemes, but a creative donor can easily find ways around the limits, for example, by paying for advertising against the opponent of the person seeking office.

In 2009, the United States Supreme Court decided *Caperton v. Massey*, the mother of all judicial fundraising cases.[25] The case received nationwide press and became the inspiration for John Grisham's best selling novel *The Appeal*. The *Caperton* case is about a guy who donated a large sum of money, not directly to a judge's campaign, but for advertising against the judge's political opponent. Caperton, CEO of a mining company, sued Massey, a coal company for cancelling a contract resulting in Caperton's company going out of business. A jury returned a verdict in favor of Caperton for $50 million. Massey appealed, and here is where it gets interesting. While the appeal was pending a colorful guy named Blankenship, who happened to be the CEO of the losing defendant coal company Massey, donated $3 million to a non-profit entity he formed. Most of the money was used in an advertising campaign *against* a sitting West Virginia Supreme Court judge named McGraw. McGraw lost the campaign and his opponent Brent Benjamin took the seat. Obviously, the Benjamin campaign was a beneficiary of the $3 million donated against his opponent. It was more than was spent by the entire Benjamin campaign. Caperton's lawyers asked Justice Benjamin to recuse himself (take himself off the case), arguing that his impartiality had been compromised by the money spent against his opponent. The judge refused the request. The West Virginia Supreme Court ruled in favor of Defendant Massey, and Justice Benjamin voted with the majority in the 3-2 decision. The case was heard again by the court the following year with the same result, and Justice Benjamin once again voted with the majority. The case then went to the United States Supreme Court which decided it in June 2009. The high court held that Justice Benjamin indeed should have recused himself. Writing for the majority, Justice Kennedy found that the conflict of interest was so extreme that it resulted in a constitutional violation of plaintiff's rights under the due process clause of the Fourteenth Amendment because there was a "probability of bias." Now remember, this was not a case of a guy approaching a judge and saying, "Hey judge, I have a case before you and by the way here's three million bucks." Before *Caperton*, the legal threshold for a judge to recuse himself was "a direct, personal, substantial, pecuniary interest" in a case.[46] This has been replaced by the "probability of bias" standard.

Chief Justice Roberts dissented, joined by Alito, Scalia, and Thomas. Justice Roberts rattled off no fewer than forty questions that a judge must now ask himself when faced with a recusal motion, including "How much money is too much."[47] In a separate dissent, Justice Scalia predicts that there is now added to "the vast arsenal of lawyerly gambits what will come to be known as the *Caperton* claim."[48]

The *Caperton* case decided, in an alarmingly vague way, when a judge should recuse himself from a case. But it will have a far reaching impact on the debate over direct political election of judges and the various merit appointment schemes. If there were no judicial elections, there would be no reason for fundraising, and all of the reasoning behind *Caperton* would become moot, except for out-and-out bribes.

Serious Money is Needed to Run for Judge

State Supreme Court candidates raised a total of $45.6 million during the 2000 judicial elections, a *61 percent increase* over the amount raised by candidates in 1998.[49] In partisan elections, the most expensive, the average raised by each candidate was $380,724 in 2000, compared to an average of $107,388 raised by supreme court candidates in nonpartisan elections. Lawyers and business groups accounted for 49% of the donations.[50]

Any lawyer who spends any time in a courtroom has been to countless fundraisers for judicial candidates. These affairs, charging anywhere from seventy-five to a few hundred bucks or more, are always packed. It's like going to a local county bar association meeting, with drinks and snacks. During election season, a serious lawyer can spend thousands of dollars at these events. Do these lawyers really care if the candidate wins? Probably not, but the felt need to make a contribution is inescapable. When you are before a judge who needs to make a call on your case, you hope he remembers that you showed up, cash in hand, at his fundraiser. "I never felt so much like a hooker down by the bus station ... as I did in a judicial race. Everyone interested in contributing has very specific interests. They mean to be buying a vote" says Paul Pfeifer, Ohio Supreme Court Justice.[51] Judicial fundraisers are very much like fundraisers for any other political office. If you have ever attended a fundraising event for a local politician, say a mayor or town supervisor, you will recall that the event was literally packed with people. Every person who does any kind of business with the entity, whether a simple building permit application or an attempt to win a municipal contract, is present. Not only are they present, but their name appears on the guest list, and that guest list is read many times. Political party affiliation doesn't matter. People show up because they want to curry favor with the candidate, who needs their money to get elected. It may seem ugly, but it is the way we do things.

Merit Selection Takes the Politics out of Picking Judges – Or Does it?

There appears to be a nationwide movement away from a simple partisan election system, with its attendant problems of fundraising, toward merit selection. Who could argue with merit selection? Is it not best for the common good to have the best people on the bench, people chosen based on merit? When you were a Boy Scout, you worked for a merit badge. When you applied to college, you hoped to get a merit scholarship. At dinners you are pleased and honored to receive a merit award. Merit – it's a great word. But the word "merit" can also be a euphemism for an old-fashioned smoke-filled room.

The Missouri Plan, also known as merit selection, was implemented in the state bearing its name in 1940 after some messy political contests for judicial spots.[52] It is really a hybrid of elections and merit appointment. A commission comes up with a list of candidates gleaned from a pool of applicants. The list is then submitted to the governor, who then picks from the submitted names. If he doesn't, the commission does the picking. In the first election held after one full year, the judges who were selected go before the voters in a *retention election.* It has been widely praised and is used in about two dozen states.

Retired United States Supreme Court Justice Sandra Day O'Connor is spearheading a nationwide effort to encourage merit selection of judges.[53] She heads the "O'Connor Judicial Selection Initiative," sponsored by a group from the University of Denver called the Institute for the Advancement of the American Legal System (IAALS). The IAALS advocates a list of six "best practices" in the selection of judges. They are:

1. Politically balanced nominating commissions with a majority of nonlawyer members making recommendations in a transparent process.

2. Appointments by the governor, who must select judges from lists provided by the nominating commissions.

3. Comprehensive judicial performance evaluations that are based on criteria such as command of the law, impartiality, and temperament.

4. Retention elections, so that voters armed with the performance evaluations can decide whether to keep the judges on the bench.

5. Terms of office that are initially only two to three years in length, so that there is sufficient data about judicial performance before the retention elections.

6. Judicial training

But does "merit selection" take the politics out of selecting judges? Does it create an unbiased system of picking the best person for the job? Does it take politics out of the equation? Maybe not.

In Missouri, for example, 17 of the last 18 nominees chosen by the Appellate Judicial Commission to fill vacancies on the Supreme Court of Missouri were Democrats, according to an organization called Better Courts for Missouri.[54] If the goal is impartiality and merit, attention must be paid to how the commissions are appointed. In Missouri, three of the seven members are lawyers from the Missouri State Bar Association. If, as opponents of the plan contend, these lawyers are "pro-plaintiff" they would need only snag one additional vote to appoint plaintiff friendly candidates. But the other commission members in Missouri are three non lawyers appointed by the governor and the Chief Judge of the state Supreme Court, who is chairman of the commission.

A major component of the merit plan is the provision for retention elections. In Missouri, there are six judicial performance evaluation committees, which circulate questionnaires among lawyers and even among jurors who have served in the last 2 years. These questions are serious, and clearly give the public an idea of how the judge has performed. The surveys, from the official Missouri courts website, are quoted here:

JUDICIAL PERFORMANCE REVIEW CRITERIA

The six judicial performance evaluation committees which analyzed the qualifications and skills of non-partisan judges seeking retention on the November 4, 2008 general election conducted their work based on a series of Judicial Performance Standards.

In making their recommendations regarding retention, the committees analyzed the results of a lawyer survey, the results of a survey of jurors, and written opinions issued by each judge.

Lawyer Survey

For *appellate judges*, lawyers were asked to evaluate judges on nine specific criteria, as follows:

1. Being fair and impartial toward each side of the case.

2. Writing opinions that are clear.

3. Writing opinions that adequately explain the basis of the court's decision.

4. Issuing opinions in a timely manner.

5. Allowing parties to present their arguments and answer.

6. Making decisions without regard to possible criticism.

7. Refraining from reaching issues that need not be decided.

8. Treating parties equally regardless of race, sex, or economic status.

9. Being courteous toward attorneys.

For *trial judges*, lawyers were asked to evaluate judges on 16 specific criteria, as follows:

1. Treats people equally regardless of race, gender, ethnicity, economic status, or any other factor.

2. Displays fairness and impartiality toward each side of the case.

3. Is not affected by partisan considerations.

4. Is prepared for hearings and trials.

5. Allows parties latitude to present their arguments.

6. Bases decisions on evidence and arguments.

7. Gives reasons for rulings.

8. Demonstrates appropriate demeanor on bench.

9. Maintains and requires proper order and decorum in the courtroom.

10. Is competent in the law.

11. Rulings on dispositive motions state reasons and consistently apply the substantive law.

12. Effectively uses pre-trial procedure to narrow and define the issues.

13. Understands rules of procedure and evidence.

14. Weighs all evidence fairly and impartially before rendering a decision.

15. Written opinions and orders are clear.

16. Clearly explains all oral decisions.

For both appellate and trial judges, lawyers' evaluations were converted into a numerical score between 1 and 5, with 1 being the poorest and 5 being the best. The number of responses and the average score is listed for each criterion.

Juror Surveys

Members of the public who had served on juries before trial judges during the last two calendar years were asked to complete a survey composed of "yes/no" answers. Questions on the juror survey are as follows:

1. Did the judge treat people equally regardless of race, gender, ethnicity, economic status, or any other factor?

2. Did the judge appear to be free from bias or prejudice?

3. Did the judge act in a dignified manner?

4. Did the judge act with patience?

5. Did the judge appear to be well-prepared for the case?

6. Did the judge clearly explain court procedure?

7. Did the judge clearly explain the legal issues of the case?

8. Did the judge maintain control over the courtroom?

9. Did the judge promote public confidence in the courts?

10. Did the judge clearly explain the responsibilities of the jury?

It is important to note that juries do not serve in appellate courts, so no jury information was involved in the evaluation of appellate judges seeking retention.

Written Opinions

Each appellate judge was asked to provide five written opinions for use by the evaluation committee. The committee was charged with the responsibility to review the decisions authored by each judge for adherence to the record, clarity of expression, logical reasoning, and application of law to the facts presented.

Each trial judge was asked to provide one written opinion for use by the evaluation committee. The committee was charged with the responsibility to review the decision authored by each judge for thoroughness of findings, clarity of expression, logical reasoning, and application of the law to the facts presented.

It's difficult to pick fault with the thoroughness of the above performance evaluation. The results of these surveys can be made available to all, including the press, when the judge runs for office in the retention election.

Negatives as well as positives are all there for all to see. Remember, the above plan is for use in retention elections, that is, an election held after the judge has sat on the bench for a year or two after having been appointed by the nominating commission and the governor. Performance criteria such as these could not be used for a person running for a judicial vacancy for the first time. Again it is a performance review for a retention election.

Which is Better – Contested Elections or Merit Selection

A major concern about merit selection schemes is that they don't take the politics out of the system, and can even make the selection process more political. In Missouri, as noted above, seventeen out of eighteen judicial appointments over a recent time period were from one party, in this case, the Democratic Party. So, the argument goes, if the Democratic (or Republican) governor appoints commission members all of similar political persuasion, the result is purely political. The solution, and it is not foolproof, is *transparency*. Why not create a system where the governor must post prospective commission members on the official state website 60 days before the person assumes the position? This gives ample time for opposition to make its voice heard, and, more importantly, for the press to analyze just what's going on. A big complaint with Missouri of recent times is that the system lacks transparency. Missouri itself seems to be having second thoughts about its namesake plan. In April 2009, the Missouri legislature approved a ballot measure that would change the way the plan works, but the initiative never made its way to a vote. A study shows that of the 50 percent of Missouri appellate court nominees who gave campaign contributions, 88 percent gave to Democrats and only 12 percent gave to Republicans.[55] Merit selection most emphatically does not take the politics out of the selection process. Lack of accountability is common complaint about merit selection. But where is the accountability in a purely political contested election? If the voters pick a judge who later turns out to be a dumb, corrupt bozo, what do they do about it? The quick answer is "vote the guy out in the next election." But that election may be many years off, leaving only impeachment as a remedy, a long and cumbersome process. Meanwhile, the incompetent judge remains on the bench to perform his handiwork. In the November 2010 election, an election marked by its anti-incumbent fervor, every one of Missouri's judges running for retention were voted back into office, with some 67% of the voters voting in favor of retention. Many commentators believe this election shows that Missouri voters are pleased with the system, but lobbyist James Harris, a long-time opponent of the Missouri plan, believes otherwise, and plans to try to get the ballot initiative reintroduced to change the plan.[56]

Does the prospect of facing the voters influence the way a judge votes? In the November 2010 election in Iowa, all three supreme court judges running for reelection were defeated, including the chief justice. The judges were part of a unanimous decision that legalized same sex marriage in the state. Interest group money flowed in from across the country for advertising against the three. All 71 judges running for lower court seats were voted in. The Iowa results brings front and center two major issues: first, will a judge's vote on a controversial issue be swayed by an upcoming election; secondly, the Iowa vote showed voter impatience with "legislating from the bench," which was a major emphasis of the ad campaigns against the judges.[57]

In Wisconsin in April 2011, what looked like an easy win for a sitting state supreme court judge turned into a hotly contested fight, because of political issues. Judge David Prosser, running for reelection, was expected to win handily against his opponent, JoAnne Kloppenburg, an assistant attorney general. But the race narrowed sharply because of the nationwide press over Wisconsin Governor Walker's attempts to curb public service union collective bargaining power by legislation. The bill passed, and the only hope for the unions appeared to be the Wisconsin Supreme Court. Prosser is a conservative, his opponent Kloppenburg a liberal. Money flowed into the race from across the country. Kloppenburg's campaign theme boiled down to "Prosser=Walker." Some of the advertising became ugly, and some nasty attacks on Prosser even suggested that he was soft on pedophilia, because of his handling of a clergy child abuse case some three decades earlier when he was a district attorney. It should be noted that the victims in that old case came to Prosser's defense. The initial poll returns on April 5 showed Kloppenburg with a razor thin lead of 205 votes out of 1.5 million. Then, to complicate matters, a tabulation error then showed that Prosser actually had a 7,300 vote lead, making him the clear winner. Because the vote is less than one-half of one-percent of the total, a recount will be held.   What is significant about this Wisconsin race is that it shows that judicial elections can indeed resemble a typical rough and tumble political brawl. Of course, neither Prosser nor his opponent came out and stated publicly how they would vote if the public union bill came before them as a case, but the clear message from both sides was that Prosser, the conservative, would be more likely than not to uphold the legislation.

There can be no doubt, and it's foolish to argue otherwise, that judicial races are political. This is especially true when the race is for the high court in any state.

But what about elections for lower court judicial seats. Judges in the lower courts do not make decisions affecting policy as do judges on the high courts. The only broad campaign issues that a lower court aspirant might put forth would be traditional slogans like "tough on crime," or a "proven record battling corruption." The candidate cannot promise how he will vote on a particular case, especially because the case is not in front of him. What gets a lower court judge elected are far more prosaic things, especially **name recognition** and **party affiliation**. Truth be told, most people enter the voting booth not having any idea who the people are who are running for judge, other than voters who personally know the candidate. Reality limits the amount a bench seeker can raise or spend to get the word out. And the "word" is limited basically to the person's resume. If one candidate can say in his campaign literature that he served 15 years in the DA's office, has a record of convicting gangsters, and has a nice family, this might be enough for a voter to cast a ballot for him. But the reality is, it is a rare chance that the average voter ever saw the candidate's literature. It got tossed in the garbage along with time-share solicitations and credit card deals.

If politics, or simply influence, plays a part in both merit selection and traditional elective politics, can we ensure that a merit selection process actually produces merit? Phrased differently, does a political system ensure lack of merit? Consider a local political leader, a "party boss," if you will. It's his job to find good (winning) candidates, raise money, and, yes, provide patronage jobs for the party faithful. Sounds all very "back roomy" doesn't it. But let's take a look at the back room. Is a local politico incentivized to select other than qualified judicial candidates? Typically, a candidate goes through a formal screening process, first by the local bar association, then by a committee of the party that makes the nomination. At no step in the process is there a bias in favor of unqualified jerks. Why should the local political leader even care who gets to be a judge, given that the judge is then separated from the political system? The judge not only can avoid future fundraisers, he is generally forbidden by ethics rules from doing so. There is a reason that the local political leader pays attention to judicial candidates – patronage. Sounds creepy, but is it really? Take, for example, the judicial office of surrogate court judge. This court presides over the distribution of property after a person dies. Kind of boring, no? No, at least not from a patronage point of view, and this is why surrogote court races are heavily funded and hotly contested. According to Mike Dawidziak, a Long Island political consultant, the surrogate's office is a "trove of patronage." There are expert witnesses to be hired, sometimes handwriting experts. There are court-appointed guardians, masters, referees and countless other little morsels to be handed out – to the party faithful. But is this wrong? Can you imagine a surrogate judge looking for people to fill those posts and putting at the top of the feeler inquiry: "Idiots only need apply." Of course not – he will look for qualified people, and yes, he will look first to those who helped get him elected. If, on the other hand, the surrogate judge was appointed he would look to – those who appointed him. Ain't democracy a bitch?

We should not let the perfect be the enemy of the good. Any attempt to completely depoliticize the system will fail. Unless computer software can be written to do the selecting, there will always be some political influence in the selection of judges.

Whether we elect or appoint our judges, one thing is certain – their compensation is very modest. In the next chapter I examine how we pay our judges.

CHAPTER 7

Judicial Compensation

A left offensive tackle in the National Football League, also known as the blindside tackle, is the second highest paid position in the league, after the quarterback. The position does not require speed. It requires a large body and brute strength. It is called the blindside because a right- handed quarterback has his back to that side when setting up to pass. The left tackle's job is to prevent his team's valuable quarterback from being blindsided, or tackled from behind, and suffer the kinetic explosion of being struck full force by a 350-pound defensive lineman. 23- year-old left tackle Michael Oher is the real-life subject of the book and movie *The Blindside.* Michael is 6 feet 4 inches tall and weighs 310 pounds. He has signed a 5-year rookie contract with the Baltimore Ravens worth over $12,500,000. Why so much? Because he's worth it. Ask his quarterback.

Chief Justice of the United States Supreme Court John Roberts earns $217,000 a year. Judith Sheindlin, the famous *Judge Judy* of daytime television, earns $45 Million a year.

The concept of "the right pay for the job" is in our American DNA. The formula for figuring out what is the right pay is dictated by the marketplace, and is made easier by the abundant data available on the Internet. It's no longer a question of speaking to your internal HR people, or calling around to a few headhunters to try to get a feel for the appropriate salary. Data crunching has replaced phone calls and reading want ads. Just look at the vast salary data from the Bureau of Labor Statistics. From that and countless other industry-specific websites, you can see who is paying what for which job. Employers know the game too. If you post a position that pays below what the market dictates – you have some explaining to do, if the phone ever rings. Efficient markets run on information, and the more information is available, the more accurate are the real numbers. Just as the market determines a stock price, the labor market sets the pay for the endless categories of positions. And the numbers show who should earn more, or less. The folks that management guru Peter Drucker named "knowledge workers" earn more than manual workers. A knowledge worker, as the name implies, labors with his mind, and uses his knowledge, both what he has and what he constantly acquires, to further the organization's mission. A computer engineer expects to earn much higher pay than a letter carrier, and the letter carrier does not begrudge him. Delivering mail is an important job in society, but there are scores of applicants who can perform that job compared to the few dweebs who can talk to the little man in the computer. It is part of our social contract. A minor league ballplayer may envy, but does not resent, Yankee slugger Alex Rodriguez's annual salary of $27,500,000, unless of course, he starts accumulating A-Rod's statistics.

High pay does not guarantee a good return on investment to be sure. Witness the debacle of a merger between AOL and Time Warner. Never before or since have so many people been paid so much money to totally screw up a basically good idea. It was to be the historic blend of new media, AOL – basically an internet service provider, with old media giant Time Warner. Ted Turner,

CNN founder and one of the principals of the deal famously said: "I did it with as much or more excitement and enthusiasm as on the night I first made love 42 years ago." After 10 unhappy years, Time Warner spun off AOL as a separate company. They should have heeded Warren Buffet: "If you were a jerk before, you'll be a bigger jerk with a billion dollars."[58]

Ignore the market, and matters can get very queer indeed. Take (or leave) the Japanese experience. Peter Drucker observed the strange results of ignoring the marketplace and substituting rigidity. "[T]he Japanese have a rule that if you finished high school you can't be a blue-collar worker, you have to be a clerk. And if you finish college, you have to be a professional or a manager. Since everybody in Japan now at least finishes high school, there is an incredible surplus of clerks and would-be managers. You know, it is unbelievable how overstaffed Japanese companies are in management."[59] We shall see later how the United States Congress has kissed off market pricing of judicial and executive salaries in favor of an arbitrary formula, linked to their own pay. If we trade the U.S. Congress for the Japanese Parliament, maybe nobody would notice.

Judicial salaries are modest, given the job requirements. A Federal District Court judge (trial judge), for example, earns $169,300 per year. A Federal Circuit Court judge (appellate judge) earns a few bucks more, $179,500 per year – about 72 percent less than young Michael Oher. Compare this to the School Superintendent of a school district on Long Island: he makes over $200,000. A more direct comparison is what a judge can earn as a senior professor at a top law school: $330,000. Or a dean: $430,000.[60] Partners at large big city law firms often earn well over one million dollars. Clearly, at the career-choosing phase of one's life, money is not a motivating factor to become a judge. Unfortunately, it is a factor that forces many judges to leave the bench. "Federal judges are overworked, underpaid and under-appreciated," says Judge Hector M. Laffitte of the District of Puerto Rico, one of the busiest courts in the First Circuit. After 23 years he is returning to private practice. Low pay is one of the major factors in his decision. "Our last pay increase was in 1989 (he is being quoted in 2007). Salary erosion is hurting judges, and I can't see an increase in our future. I've lost all hope." The lack of pay increase over the years is an important consideration. "My first year's salary as a federal judge in 1983 was essentially my expense account in private practice," says Laffitte. "But life had been good to me and I decided to give something back. I wanted to serve. I could survive because of the reserve I'd built up. But the financial nest egg has been largely used up."[61]

Chief Justice John Roberts, like his predecessor William Rehnquist, is a strong proponent of better judicial pay, and not just because he is the shepherd of the American judiciary trying to take care of his flock. He sees low judicial pay as inimical to the entire system of justice. In his 2006 *Year-End Report on the Judiciary* he warned that a judiciary restricted to "persons so wealthy that they can afford to be indifferent to the level of judicial compensation, or people for whom the judicial salary represents a pay increase...would not be the sort of Judiciary on which we have historically depended to protect the rule of law in this country." From 2000 to 2006, 38 judges left the federal bench, including 17 from 2004 to 2006. Also in the *Report* he said: "Judges who willingly make substantial sacrifices in support of public service are being asked to bear unreasonable burdens. In the face of decades of congressional inaction, many judges who must attend to their families and futures have no realistic choice except to retire from judicial service and return to private practice."

Job Security

Job security is a good thing, and the job of judging does come with significant employment safety. Whether a lifetime gig of a federal judge or a 14-year term of some state court judges (who campaign for reelection with the power of incumbency), a judge who does a reasonably good job, and avoids the limelight when he errs, can expect to keep his job. Bad judges are removed of course, but it is an arduous process.

But the job security of judges can be overstated, especially when you compare it to another secure job – teaching. A high school teacher – who works 9 months a year with lifetime tenure after a couple of years on the job – has amazing job security. Even if his students uniformly fail or move through the system by "social promotions" the one thing the teacher needs not fear is getting fired. With the power of the union behind him, it is harder to fire an underperforming teacher than to launch a satellite with a bottle rocket. Tenure, when applied to teaching could be defined as: "Learn to like him, because you're not getting rid of him." That is why principals seldom try. Three out of 30,000 teachers were dismissed for cause in New York City in 2008. In Chicago between 2005 and 2008, teachers canned for poor performance amounted to 0.1 percent, in Akron Ohio, zero percent, in Toledo, 0.01 percent and in Denver zero percent.[62]   A teachers' union is like a dragon guarding the castle. Many principals don't even bother trying to fire a clunker, fearing the lengthy and costly court battle with the dragon. And the dragon is right there at the beginning of a teaching career. Tenure is usually granted after 3 years, but in eight states it is granted after only 2 years.[63] In New York City, it is illegal to consider student test scores when making tenure decisions. So with virtually no way to evaluate a teacher's performance, tenure is granted even though a teacher's students may be failing miserably. In the documentary movie about the US education system *Waiting for Superman,* there is an almost humorous segment called "the dance of the lemons." The phrase refers to a common practice among school principals, wherein they trade off a "lemon," a bad teacher, to another school, in return for one of its lemons. The hope is that the incoming lemon won't be as bad as the outgoing one. It is that hard to get rid of a bad teacher. Don't tell judges about job security.

Www.uscourts.gov, the official website of the federal judiciary, is not shy about championing higher judicial pay. Its fact sheet is entitled "Need for Federal Judicial Pay Increase." After adjusting for inflation, from 1969 through 2006, the real pay of federal judges has actually decreased by 25%, while the average real pay of all American workers has gone up 19%. In January 2003, the National Commission on the Public Service issued a report with the startling title: *Urgent Business for America: Revitalizing the Federal Government for the 21st Century.* The commission was known as the Volcker Commission, after its chairman Paul Volcker, former

Chairman of the Federal Reserve under Presidents Carter and Reagan. This was no lightweight group. Besides Volcker it included: Charles Bowsher, former Comptroller General of the United States and head of the GAO; Bill Bradley, former Senator from New Jersey; Frank Carlucci, Secretary of Defense under Reagan; Kenneth Duberstein, former White House Chief of Staff under Reagan; Constance Horner, former Director of Personnel under President George H.W. Bush and head of Office of Personal Management under Reagan; Franklin Raines, former head of OMB under Clinton, and former CEO of Fannie Mae; Richard Ravitch, former head of New York's Urban Development Corporation and the Metropolitan Transit Authority and Lieutenant Governor of New York; Robert Rubin, former Treasury Secretary; Strobe Talbot, former head of the Brookings Institution and Deputy Secretary of State; Donna Shalala, former Secretary of HHS; and Vin Weber, former Congressman from Minnesota. The best and the brightest! Among the matters they considered in the sixty-four page report was judicial pay. While he was still Chief Justice of the United States Supreme Court, Justice Rehnquist testified before the commission. Noting that judges salaries were causing many to retire, Justice Rehnquist said: "[A]ccording to the Administrative Office of the United States Courts, more than 70 Article III judges [federal judges appointed pursuant to Article III of the United States Constitution, that is, district, circuit and supreme court judges] left the bench between 1990 and May 2002, either under the retirement statute, if eligible, or simply resigning if not, as did an additional number of bankruptcy and magistrate judges. During the 1960s on the other hand, only a handful of Article III judges retired or resigned."[64] He went on to say: "Inadequate compensation seriously compromises the judicial independence fostered by life tenure. The prospect that low salaries might force judges to return to the private sector rather than stay on the bench risks affecting judicial performance."[65] The committee went on to conclude that judicial pay is just too low and that the problem needed to be addressed immediately. "The lag in judicial salaries has gone on too long, and the potential for diminished quality in American jurisprudence is now too large. Too many of America's best lawyers have declined judicial appointments. Too many senior judges have sought private sector employment – and compensation – rather than making the important contributions we have long received from judges in senior status. Unless this is revised soon, the American people will pay a high price for the low salaries we impose on the men and women in whom we invest responsibility for the dispensation of justice."[66] The commission even made suggestions about how judges should be paid compared to other professions: "We are not suggesting that we should pay judges at levels comparable to those of the partners at our nation's most prestigious law firms. Most judges take special satisfaction in their work and in public service. The more reasonable comparisons are with the leading academic centers and not-for-profit institutions. But even those comparisons now indicate a significant shortfall in real judicial compensation that requires *immediate correction*."[67] (Emphasis added). In a section of the report entitled "Interim Steps Toward Implementation," the Volcker commission again stressed the urgency of the problem, saying that Congress' "first priority...should be an *immediate and substantial* increase in judicial salaries."[68] (Emphasis added).

"Immediate and substantial" – That should do the trick! The year after the report, federal judges got a $3,000 raise or about 2 percent. Now, over 7 years later, they get about 9 percent more than in 2003. These are not raises; these are COLAs (Cost of Living Adjustments).

Here's the problem: judges don't have a constituency of people clamoring for them to get paid more. If a poll were taken, I would wager that judicial pay is pretty far down on the average citizen's list of concerns. The commission recognized this: "It is difficult to generate public concern about the salaries of senior federal officials because those salaries are higher than the average compensation of workers nationwide."[69] And another problem about the lack of public concern is that politicians in Congress find it difficult to get juiced over an issue the public doesn't care about. It gets worse. Traditionally, Congress has linked senior government executive and judicial pay to what congressmen and senators get paid. In 1989 this linkage became a matter of statute. A senator makes what a circuit court judge makes, and a congressman gets the same salary as a district court judge. Think of the political problem. Nothing is dicier than voting oneself a raise, and therefore legislators are reluctant to do so. They defer their incomes to future book deals, speaking engagements, or lobbying jobs. Why give a political opponent a campaign soundbite. "As the people of this district are struggling to put food on the table, Congressman Bozo voted himself a raise." This is why the Volcker commission recommended that the statute be amended and that judicial and executive pay be "unlinked" to congressional pay and the political challenges that it involves. The commission recommended that executive and judicial pay be set by procedures outside of the political considerations of politicians voting themselves raises. That was over 7 years ago. Judicial and congressional pay are still joined at the hip in 2011. The problem with linkage was compounded by the infamous Section 140 which requires congressional action on cost of living adjustments to judicial salaries even if congressional salaries are not affected. The American Bar Association has recommended its repeal: "An additional source of friction results from Congress's additional power to block judicial COLAs even when it does not block an adjustment for its own Members because of the now notorious "Section 140," which was adopted as part of a continuing funding resolution in 1981 and re-enacted into law in 2003. Pursuant to "Section 140," no judicial COLA can take effect without specific authorization by Congress."[70]

In 2007, a bill was introduced in the Senate with bipartisan support called the Federal Judicial Salary Restoration Act of 2007[71]. The bill would increase a District Court judge's pay to $247,800, Circuit Court judges to $262,700, Associate Judge of the Supreme Court to $304,500 and Chief Justice of the Supreme Court to $318,200. The bill was introduced over 4 years ago. In effect it would eliminate the linkage between congressional and judicial salaries. Since then it has run into the wreckage of the Great Recession that began in December 2007. As the nation still struggles with stubborn unemployment and a tepid recovery, judicial salaries have once again sunk to the lower depths of legislative attention.

The comparison of state legislative pay to state judicial pay (unhinged or not linked to legislative pay) and congressional pay to federal judicial pay (hinged or linked to legislative pay) has broad policy implications.

It provides logical political cover to congressional leaders to say they simply are following the compensation experiments in the states, which is what federalism is supposed to be all about. By disconnecting their own pay from that of federal judges, senators and representatives will take a long step toward fulfilling their responsibility for the judicial system. The Federal Judicial Salary Restoration Act, if Congress ever gets around to enacting it., will go a long way to solving the problem.

Can judges be paid too much?

Richard A. Posner, prolific author and Judge of the Federal Circuit Court of Appeals for the Seventh Circuit has some concerns. "[O]ne effect of raising judicial salaries would be to make the job a bigger patronage plum for ex-Congressmen, friends of Senators, and others with political connections, so that the average quality of the applicant pool might actually fall."[72] He also ponders the economic principle of "opportunity cost." If a partner in a big law firm makes, say, $2 million dollars a year, and a federal judgeship pays about $170,000, the lawyer who applies for and takes the job pays a large opportunity cost. Posner worries about the gap becoming too narrow, causing leisure-loving lawyers to be attracted to the job. The job of a judge is less stressful than the travails of partnership at a big law firm, according to Posner. Because of this, the narrower the gap between a judge's pay and a law partner job, the more likely it may attract lazy lawyers. Citing a study showing the effects of compensation on judicial quality, he sees modest judicial pay as a "screening device: only lawyers who really want to be judges will accept the financial sacrifice required."[73]

He also believes that the labor pool of over one million lawyers provides a good enough group from which to select judges to replace the forty or so who retire each year, especially among those successful lawyers who have built up a substantial nest egg. Posner's views on money may be clouded, however. As one of America's leading public intellectuals, he is a prolific author, having written 28 books since 1981, about one a year. His royalty income must buffer his modest pay. He also writes all of his own opinions, lectures, and writes law review articles and articles for publications of general interest. Do you think he has ever watched a sitcom?

Bucking for a Raise

Fugetaboutit. There is nothing a judge can do to get an individual raise. It's up to the legislature. Salary adjustments are for all people in a category, and individual effort does not count. The familiar ethic of "work hard, earn more" is not part of the judicial career. It can't be. A big part of a judge's job is to keep cases moving (docket control). Suppose a judge received extra money for keeping his docket of cases under a certain number or under a percentage of all cases in a particular courthouse. For a judge to be compensated for how many cases he moves through his courtroom would pose huge ethical problems. Imagine at the end of a reporting period your case gets dismissed, making the judge eligible for a bonus. "But your honor, I'm only looking for a five-day extension to file my brief." The conflict of interest is so profound as to render the idea senseless. It's hard to imagine any of a judge's duties that could be subject to incentive pay. Quality of writing or judicial reasoning? Who decides that? Staying awake more than any other judge in the courthouse? Maintaining control over the courtroom? Judge Ito would have been docked! A judge's pay is what it is. About the only thing a judge can do is write letters to the editor, or to the chief judge, or to the legislators. So live with it, or find another job, which, unfortunately, many judges do.

The Benefits of the Job

Any career counselor who earns the title would advise a job seeker "to find something you love and are capable of doing and do it. You will have good compensation." Judges do not earn a ton of money, and becoming a judge is no way to get rich (obviously excluding corruption). But I use the word "compensation," not salary. There are benefits to the career of judging that go beyond a paycheck. A federal judge can retire at full pay at age 65 after only 15 years of service, yet many apply for senior status rather than retire. Senior status entitles a judge to receive cost of living adjustments, and since there have been only two since 1993, the incentive does not appear to be great. These people work for nothing! They could play golf, write their memoirs, or work for a law firm and make a substantial income no matter what their age. According to the official website of the United States Court System, "Senior judges do approximately 15-17 percent of the work of the federal Judiciary," said Administrative Office Director Leonidas Ralph Mecham. "In many circuits and districts, senior judges are indispensable to the proper conduct of judicial business." In fact the federal Judiciary depends on its senior judges to such a degree that if tomorrow all the senior judges decided to catch up on their lost leisure, the courts would need an additional 100 active judges to compensate for the loss of the senior judges. If Congress and the President chose not to create the new judgeships, the federal courts would grind to a halt."[74]

The site further points out the small numbers of federal judges who chose to completely retire: "Statistics show that very few federal judges—only about 1.6 percent—take full retirement before reaching 15 years of service in active status. Even fewer opt for full retirement instead of senior status when they are eligible. And a few judges, such as the late Judge Giles Rich of the Court of Appeals for the Federal Circuit, do not take senior status even when they're eligible. Rich served over 40 years as an active judge, becoming, at 95, the oldest active judge in history. Generally, however, slightly more than half of all federal judges take senior status within 1 month after becoming eligible. Seventy-five percent take senior status within a year. Slightly more than 8 percent delay the transition, working more than 20 years before taking senior status."[75]

Something else is going on here, something in the compensation of a judge that goes way beyond the paycheck.

Non-Monetary Compensation

Money is only part of any job. Sixty-five year old billionaire Larry Ellison, CEO of Oracle Corporation, the company he founded, is third on the Forbes list of the richest people, with a net worth of about $27 billion. Why does he show up for work? Why put up with the aggravation? It isn't the money. Paul McCartney, age 68 is worth over

$1 billion. He could spend his time going to concerts, not giving them. Money? I don't think so. There is also something about the profession of judging that attracts people for reasons having nothing to do with money. Let's look at the non-pecuniary attractions of judging.

- **Power**. The ability to push lawyers around and get away with it is a unique benefit, perhaps limited to the job of judging. I'm not suggesting that judges make life difficult for lawyers out of some perverse thrill (although I don't doubt this is the primary pay-off for some), but it is a function of the job. A judge needs to keep her docket moving, and this sometimes requires a very strict disciplinary approach to lawyers before the court. And what is required is not a loud voice or dominating personality; the position itself confers the power. If an attorney pushes back and tries to dominate a judge, the simple reality is that the judge can hurl all sorts of wretchedness at the non-cooperating lawyer. Especially for a judge who is assigned to handle the case the attorney is appearing on (as opposed to a judge who is temporarily assigned) the power is enormous. The judge can put the case to the bottom of the pile, order various sanctions against the attorney, including the toughest of all, hold him in contempt of court, The attorney, whose sworn duty is to his client, cannot afford to let negative feelings toward a judge in any way compromise the case. Besides the gavel suspended over the heads of over attorneys, a judge wields enormous power over litigants.

- **Prestige**. You raise your right hand, take an oath, put on a robe, and all of a sudden people stop calling you Phil or Nancy, but instead call you "Your

Honor." How cool is that? Because justice requires that we hold the dispenser of justice in a unique level of esteem, we endow that person with certain trappings: the robe; the gavel; the appelation "your honor." Depending on your docket, you may even make history. Judge Ito didn't choose to hear the Simpson trial, it was assigned to him. Judge Kenneth Rohl, an old friend of mine, since deceased, presided over the arraignment of Joseph Hazelwood, captain of the ill-fated Exon Valdez, famous for the gigantic oil spill in Alaska. He was arraigned in Suffolk County, New York because he was a resident of the county. "How was your day, Dear?" "Oh, fine. I arraigned that guy who was responsible for history's largest oil spill." For people who crave attention, a judgeship isn't a bad way to make a living.

- **Intellectual challenge.** Some judicial opinions are over 100 pages in length. It's like listening to a case and then writing a book about it. Except for the physical sciences, there are few professions that offer more intellectual stimulation than judging.

- **Lack of stress.** Every occupation involves some stress, including judging, but if we think of the job of judging as one aspect of a legal career, and compare it to the practice of law, the bench is a far less stressful place than a law office. You don't have to hustle for clients, or worry about losing a big one to the competition. But the monetary compensation of judges is too modest. Justice, not only for the members of the judiciary, but for anyone seeking it in court, demands more.

Time for Wapner – Justice in the Afternoon

TV courtroom shows have become a time-honored American entertainment genre. Judge Judy is perhaps the most famous of the current gang, and given her income of $45 Million, the most successful. The shows have been around for decades. It began in 1981 with the The People's Court and the stern but avuncular Judge Joseph Wapner. This was the first of the shows that did not use actors, but actual judges. Wapner, if you did not watch the show, was also immortalized by Dustin Hoffman's character in the movie *The Rain Man*, when the autistic Raymond would announce every day like clockwork, his favorite show: "Time for Wapner." After a successful 12-year run, Judge Wapner presided over a courtroom series involving animals with Judge Wapner's Animal Court. Other TV judge shows include Judge Joe Brown, Divorce Court, Judge Mathis, Judge Alex Ferrer, and Judge Karen.

What most of these shows have in common is that they are really arbitrations that the parties agree to be bound to, just as in traditional arbitration proceedings. The people are not actors, and the disputes are genuine. The parties agree to the arbitration contract, and the decision is enforceable in a real court as a contract. For people who love the drama of the courtroom, and have their afternoons free, their choice goes beyond Oprah.

In the next chapter I explore the daily mountain of decisions a judge makes every day.

CHAPTER 8

Judicial Decision-Making – All Day, Every Day

Making decisions is part of the deal called life – and it's often the most difficult part. Every day fills our in-box with a pile of matters that require a decision, some important, some trivial, and without the need to face these decisions, life would be an extended vacation. Because we all like vacations we often try to steal an unscheduled holiday by putting off the decision, as it can always wait until tomorrow. We take these little unscheduled vacations every day because, let's face it, making decisions is not pleasant. What if it's the wrong decision? If I do this, that might happen; if I do that, this might happen. If I do nothing today, nothing will happen – at least not today. We channel our inner Scarlett O'Hara and say: "I'll think about that tomorrow." Nothing beats a bad something, so perhaps I'll do nothing. If you don't refinance your mortgage today, interest rates won't change that much by tomorrow. Should you sell some equities and go into bonds? Heck, Warren Buffet says to ignore market timing, so there's no need to rush. Should you pay that parking ticket or fight it? Your answer date is 2 weeks from now, so put it on tomorrow's pile. Sure you have heard the familiar saying: "A decision to put off a decision *IS* a decision." Now *that's* an easy decision to make. We do this because it's easy, and usually we can get away with it without our world blowing up. It is a psychological luxury that we can afford.

Judges can't afford that luxury, although some think they can. Judges *specialize* in doing that which most of us try to avoid: make decisions. The absence of a decision is another way of saying "delay." Delay means time wasted, money spent, lives disrupted, and justice not served. Decision-making may be difficult, but it is what any judge does throughout the day. Some of these decisions can be monumental, and some merely vexing to the decision maker. But decide they must, for that is essence of the job of judging. There's even a special word for it: while we make decisions, judges *render* decisions.

Lord Eldon was an English judge famous for his inability to make a decision. He was once asked to make a decision in a case that he had heard 6 *years earlier*. He had completely forgotten about the case, and it had to be reargued. In another case he took *20 years* to decide on a will contest. Defending his famous delays he once said that he "…always thought it better to allow myself to doubt before I decided, than to expose myself to the misery, after I had decided, of doubting whether I had decided rightly and justly."[76] William Hazlitt, the great English critic and essayist, took Lord Eldon head on. He saw Eldon as a judge who "…hugs indecision to his breast and takes home a modest doubt or a nice point to solace himself with it in protracted luxurious dalliance. Delay seems, in his mind, to be of the very essence of justice. He no more hurries through a question than if no one was waiting for the result and he was merely a *dilettanti*, fanciful judge, who played at my Lord Chancellor, and busied himself with quibbles and punctilios as an idle hobby and harmless illusion."[77] Judge Eldon could have saved countless people a lot of trouble had he chosen a different occupation. Delay is not just a theoretical concern, but one that impacts everyone in the legal system, especially the public. Delay can mean months or years of torment for a couple engaged in a contentious divorce. Delay can mean vast sums of money while a business litigant awaits a judicial decision before he can return to his labors. Delay can mean nail biting anxiety for an unemployed personal injury litigant awaiting a monetary award as the bills mount up and the ability to pay shrinks. There are many reasons people want to become judges. If the willingness to make decisions, tough decisions, is not in one's list of attractive activities, he has chosen the wrong profession. His best decision would be to find another source of employment.

When a judge unreasonably delays a decision, it places the attorney in a difficult spot. Imagine yourself standing on a ferry boat with your four-year-old. He has decided to play with your car keys, and he loves to throw things. How do you coax him to "give daddy the keys"? Very carefully, very diplomatically, lest the car keys meet a watery end. The judge has your car keys. Your client badgers you daily about the state of the case, and threatens you with a Grievance Complaint to the bar association, even though you are powerless to move the matter along. Your client can't believe that the legal system works this way, and who can blame him? A while back, my barber Tony cried on my shoulder every month over a 4-year period about a judge sitting on his divorce case. This got to be scary, because Tony would curse and flail his arms about while holding his scissors and razor. Tony and his wife had no children, so there were no complicated issues of child custody. The case was, or should have been, a routine divorce matter, and there was no reason for a 4-year delay, except for the simple fact that the judge could not seem to get around to doing his job. Finally, a temporary judge was assigned to his case.

It appears that his case was not the only one receiving the glacial treatment, so the administrative judge actually assigned a temporary judge to help clear the docket. When his attorney made a plea for a final divorce decree, the temp judge looked at the file and exclaimed, "This is ridiculous." The decree was issued the next day. In other words, there was no reason why the case had been delayed for so long. But usually there is no fill-in judge to move your case, so the attorney needs to use every bit of diplomatic skill to get the judge to make a decision. There are legal remedies to force action. A *writ of mandamus* is a document that orders a public official to do something. It is rarely used on judges. No lawyer wants to receive a letter saying, in effect: "Here's my decision – I hope you like it." You won't like it.

A judge's *docket* (list of cases assigned to him), can be viewed as a file cabinet full of decisions waiting to be made. Sometimes the docket gets so lengthy it interferes with a judge's ability to make any decisions, assuming he cares. An overloaded docket is something that administrative judges frown upon, and one that makes a judge look bad in front of his peers. This is not to make light of the problems that a judge faces – some decisions are extremely difficult, and millions of dollars or a person's freedom can be at stake. One solution that many judges try is to increase staff. This is not always easy, because staffing is often not within a judge's discretion, and governmental budgets strained by economic problems don't provide an easy answer. Another way out of the docket thicket is to streamline procedures so that cases come up for disposal in an orderly fashion. But orderliness is not the stuff of court calendars, and often the best laid plans come to nothing because a complex case suddenly shows up and consumes enormous amounts of time.

Technology to the Rescue

There is specialized software available for just about any job or enterprise you can think of, and judicial docket tracking programs are no exception. These programs use database principles to keep a record of every case on a judge's calendar. But, as sophisticated as these time-saving tools are, they do not relieve a judge from the basic duty – to make the decision. Software can't over-come bad practices. Every lawyer who spends any time in the courtroom wastes a lot of that time with unnecessary appearances. Some judges are of the opinion that the annoyance of having to appear on routine matters will force attorneys to move their cases faster. This is not without some truth, but the larger truth is that many, possibly most, personal appearances by a lawyer are a complete waste of time and money. When I practiced law, my office was 35 miles from the courthouse. I would drive (70 miles round-trip) to appear on a case for which I needed an adjournment because my client was sick, and wouldn't be ready for trial the next week. This was an adjournment that any judge would readily grant. These routine appearances today could be handled by a simple e-mail application for adjournment, saving judicial time, lawyer time, and client money. If a lawyer asks for the 17th adjournment, a judge could simply deny the electronic request and demand an appearance to read the riot act to the attorney. Docket-tracking software would readily show who is foot- dragging. Sitting through a judge's morning calendar call is like watching paint dry, except paint is more colorful.

The Law Clerk

A smart judge values a good law clerk, known in some states as a law secretary. A law secretary is not to be confused with a legal secretary, an important but very different job. A law clerk or law secretary is a lawyer, and a good law clerk has many of the attributes of a judge. Ideally the law clerk should be very intelligent and capable of working under considerable stress, should be able to stand the heat, and be a good judge of character. The job of a law clerk is a great résumé enhancer, and, therefore, the hiring judge can afford to be picky. The clerk will actually act as the judge's surrogate for various conferences, including all important settlement conferences. Over time, attorneys get to know who the good clerks are, and will treat them with all the respect of a judge, short of calling them "your honor." A clerk, well versed in the law, will often write a first draft of a judge's decision. Clerks at the appellate level, and especially those at the top – United States Supreme Court clerks, should, in every sense, have the qualifications to be a judge. They should be thoroughly grounded in the law, and expert at legal research and reasoning.

But the above scenario does not always play out, and sometimes clerks are picked in advance by a political leader as a patronage job. This doesn't automatically mean that the person's qualifications are not good, just that quality may take a back seat to political considerations.

A good clerk can also help the judge to slay the docket beast. One thinks of the character Radar, the battalion clerk in the TV series *Mash*. Radar was the epitome of efficiency. The colonel would open his mouth and Radar would supply the words. He would mention something that needs to be done, and Radar would assure him that it has already been done. A good clerk can help you win a war or clear your docket. Some clerks, and the judges they work for, play good cop/bad cop. Rather than confront a lawyer directly with a disagreement, the clerk can always say: "The judge isn't going to like this." Likewise the judge can blame the clerk for being busy with an upcoming trial, saying "If you can't settle this case I don't know when it can be conferenced again." Likewise, an attorney can use the good services of the clerk to make a plea to the judge. Say he's handling a difficult divorce that has been dragging for months. If the lawyer can convince the clerk of his plight, the clerk may then go to the judge and say: "Your honor, this case has been hanging around forever – what can I do to help you to dispose of it."

Teamwork – it works everywhere.

Judicial decision-making makes the whole system move forward. Judges who put off decisions for no rational purpose should be removed from the bench.

If decision-making is a critical part of the job of judging, you may be shocked when you consider the constraints and motivations that impact those decisions. In the next chapter we look at what goes on behind the decisions.

CHAPTER 9

Constraints and Motivations of Judging

The Oxford dictionary tells us that a motivation is the reason or reasons behind one's actions or behavior. A negative motivation, a reason not to do something, is a constraint. Without motivations or constraints on our behavior, we live in a brutish state of nature where our success is determined by guile or physical domination. Motivations can be external – laws, geographical boundaries, physical limitations of strength or intelligence, or the threat of danger to name just a few. They are also internal – conscience, religious belief, shyness, reticence, or the desire to please others. Only the most severe sociopath can be said to live without internal motivations or restraints – he just doesn't care, because he is unable to care. A dictator or tyrant has few internal or external constraints. Saddam Hussein, if outfitted with a normal psyche, would not have gassed thousands of Kurds for politically expedient reasons. Stalin, one of the most murderous dictators in history, is often quoted to have said "eliminate the man, eliminate the problem." For current-day examples of rulers acting without constraints, look to almost any Middle Eastern country. The citizens are demonstrating? That's what bullets are for.

Unfettered action without any constraints is a rare thing, thank God, but there are examples strewn across the pages of history. Adolf Eichmann, the Commandant of Auschwitz and "architect of the holocaust" was a man without constraints. His husbandry of the annihilation of hundreds of thousands of Jews was a monument to

bureaucratic efficiency. That he was slaughtering innocents did not give him pause. Following orders of the
Nazi high command, he lacked external constraints, and
his lack of human decency left him without constraint in
the shadows of his own mind. Pol Pot, leader of Cambo-
dia in the mid 1970s was responsible for the death of as
many as 2.5 million people, about 21% of the population
of the country. A man without constraint. Some people
have constraints, but act as if there were none. Ponzi
Schemer Extraordinaire Bernard Madoff, a man wanting in internal constraints, acted as if external constraints
(*the law*, Bernie) did not exist, and now has 150 years of
prison time to contemplate his actions. He consented to
a lengthy interview which was published in the February
27, 2011 issue of *New York Magazine*. He doesn't deny
what he did, but places a large share of the blame on
sophisticated investors who should have known better, as well as careless regulators. It reminded me of a
criminal client I once represented who was arrested for
stealing a stereo from the front seat of a car in a parking
lot. When I visited him in jail, he seemed amazed at his
predicament, and indicated that it was the stupid victim
who really created the incident by leaving a stereo on
the front seat of an unlocked car. I almost felt guilty by
pleading him down to a misdemeanor. Some people are
seriously lacking in healthy constraints.

In a typical employer-employee relationship, the whole
system is based on rational motivations and constraints.
An employee is expected to do what his employer wants
him to do, within reason. To the extent the employee
does not do his employer's bidding, the closer he
approaches becoming a former employee. Vast library
shelves are devoted to enlightened ways for employers

to get the best results from the employee, but that is an issue of management or leadership, and does not alter the basic underpinning of the employer-employee relationship: employees answer to THE BOSS. An employee may be creative, wanting to strike out in untested areas, and may try things that go against normal procedures. An enlightened manager will encourage such diversions, being cautious that the organization's mission is not compromised. But the basic dynamic is still there – the boss decides. The constraints are economic: good job performance can result in raises and promotions. Bad performance cannot only result in lack of raises and promotions, but can also lead to termination. This is true whether the organization is unionized or not, and only the details of the constraints change. There are also non-economic constraints in a typical career. Good performance looks good in the eyes of other employees.

A constraint can be positive, as in a military setting. A constraint can keep a soldier from running away, or viewed positively, to encourage him to act with valor in pursuit of a mission. The military is keenly aware of the dynamics of "unit cohesion." Bravery in combat is a human trait that has been praised ever since thoughts were written down. The whole idea of awarding medals for valor is to encourage bravery in trying times. But behavioral scientists also see bravery as an adaptive behavior: to look good in the eyes of other soldiers. In the ethos of combat, the number one command is to support the mission, but soldiers constantly report that their primary objective is to help their buddies. "I got your back." Staff Sergeant Salvatore Giunta was the first serviceman to be awarded the Congressional Medal of Honor in the war in Afghanistan. Referring to the friends that he lost in combat, he stated in a TV interview that he would gladly return the medal if he could get his friends back. Belief in a cause, patriotism, or dedication to a mission are also internal positive constraints. In the military the hard or external constraints are to follow orders or face discipline, possibly severe. But no military force could long succeed with these hard constraints alone. During the invasion of Normandy, the Allied cause was helped by the presence among the German defenders of "Ost" (East) battalions or Ostgruppen, which consisted largely of prisoners of war from the Eastern Front. Their willingness to fight was often motivated by external constraints only ("Fight or I'll shoot you.") They surrendered in large numbers; they did not have the unit cohesion or individual motivation of a regular soldier. They lacked internal positive constraints. Internal constraints can be far more powerful than hard external constraints. In the heat of combat, running away often occurs to a soldier as a pretty good idea. External constraints (disciplinary actions, perhaps even a court martial) go only so far ("Hey, I'll hire a good lawyer"). More powerful is the gut (internal) desire to cover your friends.

In a typical employer-employee relationship, motivations and constraints abound, and form a system aimed at accomplishing the goals of the organization. The economic dynamic posits rewards – salary, benefits, raises, promotions, a career. This is what the employer provides. The employee provides her best efforts at getting the job done. The external constraints are obvious: the dangers of getting fired, not getting a promotion or raise; possibly dead-ending a career. There are also internal motivations and constraints, including the desire to appear competent in front of one's fellow employees. No one wants to appear to be a drag on the organization, not just in front of superiors but in front of colleagues. There is also the old traditional ethic born of the good feeling one gets from getting a job well done. It is not a simple case of "do it or get fired." The business section of any library is filled with books on motivating employees. A classic, Ken Blanchard's *The One Minute Manager* is a perfect example of how to surround an employee with an environment that will result in positive motivations and constraints on his behavior.[78] The book has spawned over ten other books that include "One Minute Manager" in the title. The economic relationship of employer-employee goes far beyond: "You work, you get paid." The cynical joke of the Soviet worker was: "We pretend to work; they pretend to pay us." Examine the economic carcass of Soviet Communism and the historical record overflows with the mess that occurs when there is a complete breakdown of behavioral motivation. The New Soviet Man, one who was supposed to be motivated by working to full capacity for the greater good, proved to be a figment of the Marxist imagination. An example: In America we tip. Good service = good tip. Compare the service you get in an American restaurant to the bureaucratic treatment your often get in a European restaurant. I once asked a French waiter for an extra paper napkin. He advised me that I had already gotten one. Of course I didn't tip him, but then, he didn't expect one. Motivations make the world work better.

The Motivations and Constraints of Judges

What does all this have to do with justice? Judging is the polar opposite of the normal economic relationship of employer and employee. As I discussed earlier in this book, inn the judging business, the typical employer-employee relationship is entirely different. The judge is a public employee, to be sure, and receives a paycheck from some level of government. But the usual motivations and constraints are much less than on the normal job. If you do a consistently superior job as a judge, you are not going to get a raise, nor will your excellent efforts ensure a promotion. A competent trial judge may catch the eye of those who screen for appointments to an appellate level, but it is no guarantee, nor is it even likely that trial competence gets you kicked upstairs to the appellate bench. Promotions to the appellate bench are often functions of the legislature or the executive branch or both. It would be cynical to say that competence does not count – it does – but there is a rainbow of political considerations made by people over whom the judge has absolutely no control.

Below is an examination of the common motivations and constraints of any job, compared to the job of judging.

Economic Motivation – Money and Security

As discussed previously, money is not a motivator for a judge. Because there is no such thing as performance-based pay, the financial motivation that exists in most other occupations just isn't there. But it is a regular paycheck, and the job usually includes paid vacation, sick leave, health insurance, and a pension. The lawyer's stress of marketing and making rain (finding clients) is not there, so the modest income grows in comparison to the stress of practicing law.

In other occupations money is indeed a motivator. There was a time when I would qualify that by saying that money is a motivator for seeking employment in the private sector, but since the average wage of a government employee has far outstripped the private sector, the qualifier is no longer necessary. The best example of money as a motivator was the Wall Street bonus bonanza after the financial meltdown. Arguments were made, in public with straight faces, that the huge bonuses were necessary for certain individuals because their talents were necessary to help untangle the mess (that they made).

Impressing Others

Nobody wants to look like a jerk, well, most people anyway. A judge, sitting on the bench in front of parties, spectators, court employees and lawyers, is a very public figure. Because the judge typically came from the ranks of lawyers, he really wants to impress them. This doesn't mean being a nice guy, but the desire is to impress lawyers with competency and fairness. A judge is on stage, and just like anyone in the limelight, wants to look good. A judge, especially one new to the bench, can actually be intimidated by high profile litigators, whom he knows are really a lot smarter than he is. When an F. Lee Bailey, a Robert Shapiro or a Johnnie Cochran shouts "OBJECTION" who are you to say No? Think Judge Ito.

Judges are also keenly aware of their colleagues, the other judges in the courthouse. It takes a rare individual who doesn't want to appear in a positive light before his colleagues in any organization, and this is true for judges as well. Referring to appellate judges and the "strategic theory of judicial behavior, Richard Posner states that "...judges would not always vote as they would if they did not have to worry about the reaction to their votes of other judges (whether their colleagues or the judges of a higher or lower court), legislators and the public."[79]

The Desire to do a Good Job

In any occupation, nobody wants to go home at night thinking that she botched the job that day. Commentators frequently talk about the lack of care that younger people express on the job in recent years. Old ideas such as company loyalty or simply getting the job done and doing it well are just that – old ideas. Increasingly, workers see the job as a means to an end, and quality of performance is not a prime motivator. In the judicial profession, we hope this is not true, and it probably isn't. Judging is a unique occupation, and the desire to do the job well exists, but not always. Yes, there are lazy shirkers on the bench who are just putting in the time until retirement, but only the cynic would suggest that this is a widespread problem. The trappings of the office: the announcement beginning with "Oyez, Oyez, Oyez;" the black robe; the way everybody calls you "Your Honor" – All these things are aimed to impress the public with the gravity of the proceedings, but the effect is felt by the judge as well.

Avoiding reversal on appeal

Cases get reversed or modified on appeal all the time. But some judges seem not to care if their decisions meet with appellate disapproval. This is so for both trial judges and intermediary appellate courts. In the 2009 term of the United States Supreme Court, the Ninth Circuit Court of Appeals was reversed in 15 of the 16 cases that went up to the high court.[80] Some refer to the Ninth Circuit as the Ninth *Circus*. Being reversed can be embarrassing and some judges are extremely "reversal averse," and write their decisions with a goal not to get overturned by the appellate court. The Ninth Circuit seems to take reversal as a badge of honor.

Preconceived Notions

A preconceived notion is a constraint on a judge that may not even rise to the level of a conscious thought. A judge cannot ignore subconscious beliefs any more than anyone else. The only difference may be that a judge should be keenly aware that hard-wired beliefs should not interfere with the sworn duty to the law. But that is a lot easier said than done. From the moment of birth we are exposed to an immeasurable amount of stimuli, positive and negative. Some of the conclusions we make, and the decisions we render, are the result of early childhood experiences of which we have no recall. Sometimes we have an immediate dislike for someone, who may subconsciously remind us of a childhood bully. The Roman poet Ovid said it well: "*Non amo te, Sabidi; nec possum dicere quare; hoc tantum possum dicere, non amo te.*" (I don't like you Sabidi, and I can't say why; this only can I say, I don't like you).[81] If Sabidi is before a judge who holds this opinion of him, he is in for a very long day. Prejudices, hang-ups, and preconceived notions are something we have to live with, and so do judges. Nobody can control something of which they are unaware, but justice demands that we make an effort to ferret out these subconscious beliefs or prejudices. If a judge notices that he doesn't like people named Sabidi, he should make every effort to keep that in mind, and possibly recuse himself from a case if he can't shake it. Judges are human.

The judicial profession is unlike most others, and the comparisons only serve to highlight that fact. Judges are the primary agents for delivering justice in America, and their motivations affect the workings of the law like no other job.

In the next chapter we'll see how a common affliction can be totally unacceptable on the bench – nodding off.

CHAPTER 10

Sleeping on the Bench:
The Jury has Heard the Evidence.

It's 3 PM on the day 11 of a jury trial involving a patent infringement case. Plaintiff corporation claims that a former executive has stolen trade secrets involving a light switch that turns off lights after a period of time. Defendant claims that his switch only turns half the distance of plaintiff's switch, and therefore is a different technology. Defendant's seventh expert witness is being cross-examined and has been on the stand for 45 minutes. The judge is lying down on a large yellow marshmallow in the middle of the ocean while his nose is being licked by a Shi-Tzu puppy. The sea is calm, so the marshmallow rocks gently. Seagulls circle gracefully, outlined against the cloudless blue sky. In a window rattling voice (trial lawyers are trained to do this – It's a style thing), plaintiff's counsel shouts "OBJECTION, YOUR HONOR." Thus begins *The Awakening* in three parts. Part 1 – In a zillionth of a second a lightening bolt crosses between two brain synapses and causes the judge to ponder: "Why would anyone object to such a cute puppy licking my nose"? Part 2 – Thunder follows the lightening, with an incoming snorty snore, the force of which vibrates the epiglottis (the little tear-shaped thingy at the back of your throat) like Mike Tyson working a punching bag, and the sound of which is like a crocodile ingesting a pig, and is simultaneously followed by a vertical up-snap of the head and an opening of the eyes. Part 3 of *The Awakening* is a prayer, which, regardless of one's religious leanings is always a variation of: "Dear God, what am I doing here, who are these people, and why are they staring at me"? An experienced trial lawyer will often ignore the awakening, lest he incur the wrath of a person who is very important to his client's case. This can be a problem, however, if the judge's sleeping can become part of the evidence for appeal. An experienced judge will also ignore his awakening (What's a guy to do, apologize for falling asleep?) In response to the attorney's loud objection, he will usually issue the customary: "The jury has heard the evidence counselor." Now one of two things will happen. The attorney will either sit down (a clear indication that he didn't think his objection had much strength anyway), or he will ask: "Your honor, may we approach the bench."? "Good deal" thinks the judge. "This guy will explain his objection, and now that I'm awake I can make a sound ruling and avoid being reversed on appeal." This is how the mind works when aroused from inappropriate slumber.

In The Republic, Plato warned us:"…how far better it is to arrange one's life so that one has no need of a judge dozing on the bench."[82]

I am not picking on judges here. Falling asleep during boring testimony is probably a very normal human reaction to the surrounding stimuli. Witnesses are called, not for their oratorical skills but for what they know or have seen. The participants in a trial are not there to put on a dramatic performance. A monotone voice can challenge the most agile mind to stay focused. But it may not be a simple case of boring testimony. I once saw a person fall asleep at a basketball game! Beyond boredom is the serious possibility of a medical condition such as sleep apnea or narcolepsy. Sleep apnea means "cessation of breath" caused by airway obstruction during sleep and can result in daytime fatigue and drowsiness.[83]   Narcolepsy is a very serious medical condition characterized by overwhelming and constant fatigue and sleepiness.[84] About one in 2000 Americans suffer from it. Any judge who has problems staying awake should seek medical help to see if there is a serious underlying condition. These conditions can be reversed or at least ameliorated. We are bombarded with advertising about treatments for sleep disorders. It's a common problem. But, when a judge has the problem, it is not just his problem, but a problem for anyone who depends on his decisions and actions. A drowsy judge in Australia became the focus of a media feeding frenzy.   The Australian newspaper the *Daily Telegraph* ran 18 articles, 3 editorials, and 3 editorial cartoons in a 6-week period.[85] Dubbed "Judge Nodd," his real name is Ian Dodd. He once was reported to have fallen asleep during a rape victim's testimony. In a drug smuggling trial, jurors complained of his loud snoring. Attorneys would regularly pass notes to a clerk near the bench to nudge the judge. The irony is, prior to the media outburst, he had been diagnosed with obstructive sleep apnea and received treatment. After his treatment, there were no further reports of him sleeping. He retired in 2005 with a pension, and avoided an investigation by the Judicial Commission. He woke up just in time.

If there is no underlying medical condition, the obvious answer for the judge is to take a careful look at his or her habits, including diet and exercise. A judge spends a lot of time sitting and the brain needs oxygen, which exercise provides. Any job that requires mental acuity and good judgment requires physical health. A neighbor of mine was at our house for a barbecue. His engineering company customizes high performance engines for racing boats. He also personally tests the newly outfitted boats on the water. When I offered him a drink he declined. I asked him if he was a teetotaler. He explained: "When I'm on the water doing 120 miles per hour I want to have every wit available to me." Sober as a judge!

The problem with a judge falling asleep is obvious: a judge has enormous power – even involving life and death – and needs to be aware of everything that goes on in the courtroom. Chief Justice John Roberts, during his confirmation hearings before the Senate Judiciary Committee famously said: "Judges are like umpires. Umpires don't make the rules; they apply them. They make sure everybody plays by the rules. But it is a limited role."[86] A trial judge is not just *an* umpire, but *the* umpire for all the bases and the outfield. Sleeping should not be an option but it often happens, and when it does, justice is not only blind but deaf and dumb. Consider a criminal trial where the accused faces a lengthy sentence. If a judge sleeps through key testimony or allows in faulty evidence, the result can be decades of incarceration for the defendant. Here is where things get very sticky for the lawyers. For an appeal to be successful there must be a record of what happened at trial. An appellate brief must be attached to the transcript of the trial, and each item appealed must be noted in the record by page number. An appeal is not the place to argue: "Oh by the way, the judge slept through half the trial – *trust me*." Should the attorney object each time the judge nods off, thereby preserving the record for appeal? Tough call. If he doesn't object, there is no basis in the record from which to appeal. If he does object, he risks alienating the judge. Even if a record is made of each instance of judicial napping, the attorney handling the appeal must show that the sleeping affected the outcome, a difficult task. A New Hampshire Judge, Patricia Coffey, slept during a trial that resulted in a 23- year prison sentence. A complaint was filed by the defendant's wife, and her allegations were confirmed by two jurors. She was subsequently found in violation of the judicial code by a committee on judicial conduct. Jack King, director of public affairs for the National Association of Criminal Defense Lawyers told New Hampshire Public Radio: "Somebody has to say for the record, 'I hate to interrupt here but the judge appears to have fallen asleep. If he is just leaning back with his eyes closed, he will jump up and say I am not asleep. But if he is asleep he's not going to say anything – and it will go into the record and the court of appeals will have to decide whether or not he was asleep during some non-consequential testimony or some crucial testimony."[87]

Former Michigan Supreme Court Chief Judge Clifford Taylor was the subject of a political attack ad accusing him of sleeping during oral arguments in a case involving six kids killed in an electrical fire. The underlying lawsuit was against the City of Detroit and its housing commission. The Michigan Supreme Court held 4-3 with Judge Taylor in the majority that defendants were immune from suit. The video, with the tagline, "The Fairy Tale of the Sleeping Judge" shows a look-alike actor portraying the judge nodding off, with an overlay of the parent of the children saying that Taylor slept. Sponsored by the state Democratic Party, the ad received huge media attention and became known as the "Sleeping judge" video. It appears on YouTube. There was considerable controversy over whether he did actually fall asleep. One of the attorneys on the case was taking notes and observing the demeanor of the judges on the bench, a typical task of an appellate lawyer. He stated that he saw no judge nodding off and certainly would have noticed if they had. The complaint was filed and the ad appeared 1 year after the case was decided and *1 month before the election.* Nevertheless, Justice Taylor was defeated for reelection, the first time a sitting Chief Justice lost a race in Michigan. The voters were obviously convinced by the ad.

Lady Justice may wear a blindfold, but she is not asleep.

In the next chapter, I examine the doctrines of the Supreme Court of the United States. The strained constitutional interpretation of some of the cases might lead one to conclude that some of the justices *must* have been asleep.

CHAPTER 11

The Law of the Land –
The Supreme Court and its Doctrines

This chapter is not a review of Constitutional law to date, but is intended to highlight some critical areas of law that the United States Supreme Court has addressed over the years. The United States Supreme Court is the final say, the ultimate decider of the law in our country. Once a decision is rendered, that's it. Recall the amazing days of *Bush v. Gore*, the legal proceedings that determined who would be President of the United States. The decision, which resulted in the election of George W. Bush, was criticized in many circles, and still is. Books have been written about it. But that doesn't matter – the decision was made, and it was final.

Economic Interests

In 2001, a couple of Oklahoma business partners, scratching the entrepreneurial itch caused by the Internet, came up with a neat business idea: Why not sell funeral caskets online? After all, you can buy cars, houses, TVs, and countless items over the WEB, so why not caskets? Using the efficiencies of the internet, they could not only make a buck, but give the consumer more choice. This was to be a classic all-American blending of the old economy (skilled carpentry and manufacturing processes) and the new economy (the Internet). Anyone who has lost a loved one is familiar with the sad custom of visiting a funeral home, viewing the casket offerings in a display room, and making the often difficult choice. It seldom occurs to anyone to go out and shop for a casket, looking for the best price and a wide selection. No, you make your choice and place your order right there. The couple, Kim Powers and Dennis Bridges, decided to change the way of doing things, at least in Oklahoma. Thus was born Memorial Concepts Online, Inc. A great idea, yes? The Oklahoma State Board of Embalmers and Funeral Directors didn't think so, and they had the law on their side. Note that selling caskets is a large part of the income stream in the funeral business. It seems there is a statute in Oklahoma that requires a person wanting to sell caskets to first become a licensed funeral director. This requires 60 credit hours of undergraduate training, a one-year apprenticeship, including the embalming of 25 corpses, and a written exam. Once you have your license, in order to sell caskets, you need a fixed location, a body-preparation room, a showroom with at least five coffins, and a room for public viewing of the body. This is such a regulatory hurdle as to make it practical nonsense to want to sell caskets online. Try Pez dispensers instead. To a person unfamiliar with Constitutional Law, it would appear that this Oklahoma statute is just not rational, that it couldn't pass a thing called the "rational basis test," which is one of the tests a court uses to see if legislation is constitutionally proper. Casket-making requires carpentry or metal fabricating skills and has nothing to do with the actual interring of a body

On its face, law appears insane. What public good could the legislature have had in mind by requiring carpenters and metal fabricators to become funeral directors? After trial, the Federal District Court Judge found in favor of the funeral board and against plaintiffs. His decision was affirmed on appeal by the appellate Circuit Court.[88] The United States Supreme Court refused to hear the case. You want to sell caskets in Oklahoma? Invest a few years of your life and become a funeral director. But if there is anything shocking about this case, it is that it is simply not shocking. Both the trial judge and the appellate court were correct in their decisions. This was not a case of an activist judge or legislating from the bench or a judge making a decision based on personal beliefs. This was simply a case where the judiciary *applied the law to the facts* – a routine decision, actually. The law is completely settled, and the decision had to go to the defendant Board of Embalmers and Funeral Directors. To a lay person, and to many lawyers and judges, this outcome seems just plain wrong. Making caskets has nothing to do with burying bodies. But that is irrelevant and its irrelevance goes to the heart of one of the greatest problems in American democracy: Legislatures, federal and state, have a blank check to control individual economic interests.

The problem exists right in our Constitution, or rather in the way the Constitution has been interpreted by the Supreme Court. There was a great debate before the ratification of the Constitution in 1787 as to what individual rights should be specified. The answer came in the Bill of Rights consisting of the First Ten Amendments, ratified in 1791. The first eight of those amendments are known as the *enumerated rights*, that is, specific rights such as the right to free speech in the First Amendment.

The Ninth Amendment was included as a sort of catch-all for all those rights of the people not specifically enumerated in the first eight. The Ninth Amendment reads: "The enumeration in the Constitution, of certain rights, shall not be construed to deny or disparage others retained by the people."[89]   It was an expression of the idea that not every right could be specifically enumerated in the Constitution, but that the document did not exhaust the entire realm of just what are "rights."   It's sort of like the words you see in a contract "Including but not limited to." The Ninth Amendment suffers from lack of respect, perhaps owing to its intentional and annoying vagueness.   Conservative scholar and judge Robert Bork, in his unsuccessful confirmation hearings as a Supreme Court justice before the United States Senate, referred to the Ninth Amendment as an "inkblot," meaning that if you replaced it with an inkblot, the blot itself would give the reader no more help in deciphering its meaning than the words itself.   But it is clear that the Ninth Amendment showed that the Framers were uncomfortable with the idea that the First Ten amendments totally exhausted the concept of rights.   Does the Ninth Amendment contemplate the right, for example, to make a living? Well, yes and no.

In the early 1930s a Mr. Nebbia decided that he could sell milk cheaply. The problem was that his actions violated the dictates of the New York Milk Control Board, which was empowered, among other things, to set the price of milk, and he was convicted of a crime. The Supreme Court upheld his conviction, finding that: "[A] state is free to adopt whatever economic policy may be reasonably deemed to promote public welfare, and to enforce that policy by legislation adapted to its purpose. The courts are without authority either to declare such policy, or, when it is declared by the legislature, to override it. If the laws passed are seen to have a reasonable relation to a proper legislative purpose, and are neither arbitrary nor discriminatory, the requirements of due process are satisfied...."[90] As the dissent pointed out: "He was convicted of a crime for selling his own property – wholesome milk – in the ordinary course of business at a price satisfactory to himself and the customer."[91] "The right to an honest living, gutted in *Nebbia*, had been recognized in one form or another as far back as the Magna Carta."[92]

The Rational Basis Test Replaces the "Puke Test"

It gets worse. In the *Carolene Products* case from 1938, a case also involving milk, the Supreme Court reversed a lower appellate court and upheld the constitutionality of the Federal Filled Milk Act. Defendant sold milk at a discount that was "filled" with products other than milk, such as vegetable oil. The Court found: "...the existence of facts supporting the legislative judgment are to be presumed, for regulatory legislation affecting ordinary commercial transactions is not to be pronounced unconstitutional unless in the light of facts made known or generally assumed it is of such a character as to preclude the assumption that it rests upon some rational basis without the knowledge and experience of the legislators."[93] This became known as the ***rational basis test***, and has controlled court decisions on legislation ever since. Before this, Oliver Wendell Holmes used to apply a "Puke test;" that a statute is unconstitutional only if it makes you want to throw up.[94] The *Carolene Products* decision was only 10 pages, but a footnote in the case became the most famous footnote in constitutional law, and perhaps in American history. In Footnote Four, Chief Justice Stone gave some additional thoughts, a sort of "by the way,' known to lawyers and judges as *dicta* – something that is not critical to the outcome or decision in the case. He stated:

"There may be narrower scope for operation of the presumption of constitutionality when *legislation appears on its face to be within a specific prohibition of the Constitution*, such as those of the first ten amendments, which are deemed equally specific when held to be embraced within the Fourteenth.... It is unnecessary to consider now whether legislation which restricts those political processes which can ordinarily be expected to bring about repeal of undesirable legislation, is to be subjected to more exacting judicial scrutiny under the general prohibitions of the Fourteenth Amendment than are most other types of legislation. Nor need we inquire whether similar considerations enter into the review of statutes directed at particular religious ... or national ... or racial minorities ...: whether prejudice against *discrete and insular minorities* may be a special condition, which tends seriously to curtail the operation of those political processes ordinarily to be relied upon to protect minorities, and which may call for a correspondingly more searching judicial inquiry."[95]

In other words, if the complained rights violation is one of the enumerated rights in the first eight amendments it will get a "more searching judicial inquiry." This distinction, announced in an unnecessary footnote, eventually became law of the land. There are now two levels of judicial scrutiny when examining whether legislative action is unconstitutional: If the legislation involves a fundamental enumerated right, such as found in the first eight amendments, the court will apply strict scrutiny and will overturn a statute if it does not serve a *compelling state interest*. If the legislation does not involve a fundamental right, such as many economic "rights" including the right to earn a living, it will be analyzed using a rational basis. If the legislator had a rational basis and a legitimate state interest, the law will not be found unconstitutional. In a way, this doctrine has made a judge's job a lot easier. If a litigant complains that his rights were violated by a legislative act, and those rights are not in the Bill of Rights, then, with the flick of the memorized text key on his word processor, the judge can insert an opinion finding that there is a rational basis, legitimate state interest, and it is not his job to second guess the legislature, blah, blah, blah. Over the years case by case, brick by brick, precedent by precedent the courts have refused to upset legislative enactments under the rational basis test. The rational basis test is a very low threshold. Often, court opinions will precede the phrase with "any" or "mere," as in: We are only required to find whether the legislature acted with (any or mere) rational basis, and this court will not substitute its opinion for that of the legislature." So a statute can be stupid, ill-conceived, bizarre or just plain nuts. But it only has to have a *rational basis.*

The Rational Basis Parlor Game

To explain the rational basis test, I have come up with a parlor game that I recommend to law students, lawyers and judges, especially new judges. It goes like this: Each player has to write a statute that he or she believes will be constitutionally invalidated under the *rational basis test*. The majority of the players, acting as judges, will make each determination. I could only come up with one. Recall the Woody Allen movie, *Bananas*, wherein the people of a small republic were fed up with their nasty dictator and replaced him with a new leader, only to find out that the new guy was a bigger nutcase than the one they deposed. His first act was to announce a new law requiring all citizens to change their underwear every half-hour, and to wear the undergarments *on the outside* so the authorities can check.[96] I vote it's a winner. What rational basis in favor of what legitimate state interest could such a crazy law serve? I may be wrong. I can imagine a judge somewhere saying: "Who am I to determine that underwear should be worn on the inside? It's for the legislature to decide." As long as non-fundamental right cases – primarily economic ones – are constitutionally analyzed under the hands-off rational basis test, state and federal legislators have carte blanche to regulate commercial activity. Many Supreme Court doctrines such as the rational basis test, began during the Progressive Era, and were aimed at correcting serious societal ills, such as dangerous working environments, oligarchic control over labor by trusts, and disparate treatment of minorities. But in the nature of pendulums, the swing has been very far. These ills did exist and called for correction, but bashing the Constitution into an incomprehensible mess was not the answer.

The Interstate Commerce Clause – The Expansion of Federal Power

U.S. Constitution Article 1, Section 8, Paragraph 3 empowers Congress: "To regulate Commerce with foreign Nations, and *among the several States*, and with the Indian Tribes (emphasis added)." This is the Commerce Clause, and the words in bold have become known as the

Interstate Commerce Clause. What could be more logical than to give the Congress the power to ensure that commerce works properly between the states of the union? On its face it appears simple, noncontroversial, and a blunt statement of a power that a federal government needs in a republic. Our system wouldn't work if states were allowed to enact border tarrifs, fees, or erect security gates at the border of a neighboring state. The new nation needed a healthy economy, and that meant that commerce needed to flow freely between the states. Under the old Articles of Confederation there were serious problems with commerce between the states, some of which printed their own currency and enacted tariffs.[97] The Anti-Federalists, who initially opposed ratifying the Constitution, were troubled by Congressional control of the militia and especially by the power to raise a standing army, both possible sources of potential tyranny, but the commerce clause didn't seem to bother anybody. "To regulate commerce...among the several states" seems harmless. But the clause has been used to expand the role of the federal government in directions never envisioned by the framers. The Tenth Amendment clearly sets forth the limited delegated power of the federal government: "The powers not delegated to the United States by the Constitution, nor prohibited by it to the States, are reserved to the States respectively, or to the people."[98]

There was very little discussion of the Commerce Clause in the first hundred years of its existence, until the 1930s. A dramatic shift occurred in *National Labor Relations Board v. Jones & Loughlin Steel*. In that case, the court started to give great elasticity to the apparently simple dictate of the commerce clause, expanding the concept of what is *inter*state (between states) versus *intra*state (within a state) commerce. In upholding the constitutionality of the

National Labor Relations Act, the court held: "Although activities may be intrastate in character when separately considered, if they have such a *close and substantial relation to interstate commerce* that their control is essential or appropriate to protect that commerce from burdens and obstructions, Congress cannot be denied the power to exercise that control."[99] No longer was the commerce clause limited to trade between the states, but included agriculture, manufacturing, and production that was intended for interstate trade. The foundation had been laid for an historic and ongoing expansion of federal power. The wraps were taken off 5 years later in a decision that turned the commerce clause inside out. In *Wickard v. Filburn* the Court allowed federal regulation of a product that came from purely local production, whether or not it was even intended for interstate trade.[100] The facts under which the case arose began during the depression. To keep up and stabilize the price of wheat, Congress enacted the Agricultural Adjustment Act of 1938, which limited the amount of wheat a farmer could produce per acre, thereby driving up its price. Roscoe Filburn was growing wheat to feed his own chickens, using the rest for his family and a small amount for sale locally. He was fined $117 and was ordered to destroy his crops. What Filburn engaged in was not commerce, but agricultural production, and it was not interstate but local. The Court didn't restrict itself to the evidence in the trial transcript, but speculated on what the legislators *may* have considered. "[We have] no doubt that Congress may properly have considered what wheat consumed on the farm were grown, if wholly outside the scheme of regulation, would have a substantial effect in defeating and obstructing its purpose to stimulate trade therein at increased prices."[101]

Note: "...what Congress *may properly have considered*...." The Court might as well have taken a razor blade and removed the Interstate Commerce Clause from the Constitution, but instead it took the plain meaning of the text and rendered it meaningless. Federal power took off and never looked back. The consequences are enormous, especially in criminal law. Robert Levy and William Mellor state the problem well.

> For more than fifty years following *Wickard*, no law was ever struck down for exceeding Congress's power under the Commerce Clause. The Interstate Commerce Clause became and remains the primary source of federal power. Among the many consequences of this shift has been the massive federalization of traditional state functions, particularly in the area of criminal law – absurdly characterized as regulation of interstate commerce. This trend has been so widespread that no one seems sure exactly how many federal criminal laws exist. One recent estimate suggests that there are more than four thousand federal statutory crimes covering an unimaginable variety of activities from the most heinous crimes to the misuse of the "Smokey Bear" character or name. The number of federal regulations that may be enforced criminally is even more difficult to quantify, with estimates ranging from ten thousand to three hundred thousand.[102]

The roaring engine of federal power briefly sputtered in 1995, and again in 2000. In *United States v. Lopez* the Supreme Court faced the issue whether a student's possession of a firearm and ammunition constituted "commerce" under the Interstate Commerce Clause. The twelfth grade student was found in possession of a .38 caliber gun and five bullets. He was charged with violating the federal Gun Free School Zone Act of 1990. A Texas law also prohibited this activity, but the charges were dropped when the federal case commenced. The government's argument was that guns are dangerous and upset a school's basic mission which is to educate children. Hard to argue with that. But the government went on to argue that a poor education will result in lower grades, which will impact a kid's economic future, which may involve interstate commerce. *Enough already*, held the Chief. Writing for the majority, Chief Justice Rehnquist spelled out the limits of the Commerce Clause. "To uphold the Government's contentions here, [the Court] would have to pile inference upon inference in a manner that would bid fair to convert congressional authority under the Commerce Clause to a general police power of the sort retained by the states."[103] In 2000 the Court once again noticed that there might be some plain meaning to the Commerce Clause. *United States v. Morrison* concerned the constitutionality of the federal Violence Against Women Act of 1994, and whether it was allowed by the Commerce Clause. Again writing for the Court, Chief Justice Rehnquist wrote: "Gender-motivated crimes of violence are not, in any sense of the phrase, economic activity."[104] "We rejected these "costs of crime" and 'national productivity' arguments because they would permit Congress to 'regulate not only all violent crime, but all activities that might lead to violent crime, regardless of how tenuously they relate to interstate commerce.'[105] We noted that, under this but-for reasoning: 'Congress could regulate any activity that it found was related to the economic productivity of individual citizens: family law (including marriage, divorce, and child custody), for example.

Under the[se] theories . . . , it is difficult to perceive any limitation on federal power, even in areas such as criminal law enforcement or education where States historically have been sovereign. Thus, if we were to accept the Government's arguments, we are hard pressed to posit any activity by an individual that Congress is without power to regulate'"[106] So it would appear that a bright new day had dawned on the plain text of the Constitution in the Commerce Clause.

It got dark again – fast. Neither *Lopez* nor *Morrison* overruled the *Wickard* case; they merely distinguished it on the basis that *Wickard* involved "economic" activity.

In 2005, the Court made it clear that *Wickard* was still the law of the land on the issue of the Commerce Clause, and that the notion of economic activity is as elastic as a rubber band. In *Gonzales v. Raich* a couple of women grew and consumed marijuana for medical use under a doctor's prescription, following California's Compassionate Use Act, and thereby running afoul of the federal Controlled Substances Act.[107] Apparently unaware of Oliver Wendell Holmes' *Puke Test*,[108] Justice John Paul Stevens wrote: "In *Wickard*, we had no difficulty concluding that Congress had a rational basis for believing that, when viewed in the aggregate, leaving home-consumed wheat outside the regulatory scheme would have a substantial influence on price and market conditions. Here, too, Congress had a rational basis for concluding that leaving home-consumed marijuana outside federal control would similarly affect price and market conditions."[109]

Indulge me if you will, while I fantasize Woody Allen's dictator's Placement-of-Underwear Act on this court's docket.[110] Justice Sandra Day O'Connor dissented, finding no material distinction between this case and *Lopez* or *Morrison*. She zeroed in on whatever is left of the concept of economic activity. "The Court's definition of economic activity is breathtaking. It defines as economic any activity involving the production, distribution, and consumption of commodities. And it appears to reason that when an interstate market for a commodity exists, regulating the intrastate manufacture or possession of that commodity is constitutional either because that intrastate activity is itself economic, or because regulating it is a rational part of regulating its market."[111] Justice O'Connor also gave a succinct nod to the very reason for our system of federalism. "One of federalism's chief virtues, of course, is that it promotes innovation by allowing for the possibility that 'a single courageous State may, if its citizens choose, serve as a laboratory; and try novel social and economic experiments without risk to the rest of the country.'"[112] She also stated the obvious: "If the Court always defers to Congress as it does today, little may be left to the notion of enumerated powers."[113]

In the near future, the Commerce Clause will be in for a real Jane Fonda workout. In March 2010, Congress passed the Patient Protection and Affordable Care Act, popularly known as Obomacare. One of the provisions of the act is headed toward a collision with the Commerce Clause. The act provides that all citizens will be required to purchase health insurance or be fined. In at least one decision on the act already, Federal District Court Judge George Steeh found that the law did not violate the Commerce Clause because "by choosing to forgo insurance [the challengers] are making an economic decision to try to pay for health care services later, out of pocket, rather than now through the purchase of insurance, collectively shifting billions of dollars, $43 billion in 2008, onto other market participants."[114] In other words, a decision not to buy insurance (which seems a lot like "inactivity") has been construed to mean an economic activity, subject to regulation by Congress.

In the interest of intellectual honesty, I suggest the following press release for the Supreme Court's consideration:

FOR IMMEDIATE RELEASE

We Justices of the Supreme Court, and speaking for our brethren going all the way back to our holding in the *Wickard* case in 1942, hereby state that we really don't like the so called Commerce Clause the way it is plainly written, and we apologize for all the confusion over the years caused by our trashing of the English language in trying to make the Clause what we really want it to be. Therefore, the word "commerce," in Article 1 Sect 8, paragraph 3 is hereby deleted and is replaced by the following phrase: "whatever Congress or its vast army of delegates in countless federal agencies would like to regulate." Therefore, the Commerce Clause (whoever named it the Commerce Clause anyway?) shall now read: "Congress shall have the power…To regulate whatever Congress or its vast army of delegates in countless federal agencies would like to regulate." We realize that the United States Constitution is pretty specific as to how it can be amended. Article 5 includes all those nettlesome details about two-thirds of the state legislators making a proposal, then you need a convention, then you need three fourths of the states to ratify – All very bothersome stuff.

So therefore we have decided to amend it on our own – Hell, we've been doing it for over 70 years with word games. This amendment will do away with all that endless yackety-yak about enumerated powers, federal system, rights reserved and such. We realize that some Neanderthal strict constructionists with their hang-ups about textualism might object to this method of amendment. So what. In the words of former House Speaker Pelosi: "We have the votes."

Eminent Domain – Government's Power to Take Private Property

"...nor shall property be taken for public use without just compensation." U.S. Constitution Fifth Amendment.

The taking of property for public use is a necessary power of any government at any level. Without the power, there could be no public roads, parks, utility easements or other public uses. The big question of just what is public use came before the Supreme Court in 2005 with *Kelo v. City of New London*, one of the most controversial decisions in recent memory.[115] The City of New London determined that an area of the city, Fort Trumbull, needed to be revitalized and redeveloped to fit in with the plans of drug giant Pfizer, Inc. which intended to create a large nearby research facility. The city condemned the property of plaintiff Kelo and four others who did not want to sell their property. The area in question was by no means blighted, or even run-down. It just got in the way of a redevelopment plan. The area in question was about 5 1/2 acres out of a total of 90 acres. Plaintiffs argued that the plan would take their private property and transfer it to another private entity, the developer, and that this did not constitute a public use. The 5-4 majority, with Justice Kennedy providing the swing vote, held in favor of the city, finding that the action constituted a public use. In her strong dissent, joined by Justices Scalia and Thomas, Justice O'Connor stated:

> Under the banner of economic development, all private property is now vulnerable to being taken and transferred to another private owner, so long as it might be upgraded—*i. e.,* given to an owner who will use it in a way that the legislature deems more beneficial to the public—in the process. To reason, as the Court does, that the incidental public benefits resulting from the subsequent ordinary use of private property render economic development takings "for public use" is to wash out any distinction between private and public use of property—and thereby effectively to delete the words "for public use" from the Takings Clause of the Fifth Amendment.[116]

One commentator estimated that in the first year after the *Kelo* decision local governments used the threat or actually did condemn over 5,683 private parcels for transfer to other private parties.[117] This shows the enormous power of a Supreme Court decision. Since the founding of the republic, all levels of government operated on the assumption that the taking of property for public use, actually meant for public use. Public use meant roads, utility easements, military installations, and the like. Nobody thought that a public use could mean a private use that government, in its wisdom, determines to be a better use than the current one. Judge Richard Posner takes an interesting view of the case, finding the decision pragmatic because the storm of controversy the case unleashed resulted in a very democratic response: "Paradoxically, the strong adverse public and legislative reactions to the Kelo decision are evidence of its pragmatic soundness (Posner is considered the leader of the pragmatic school of decision-making). When the court declines to invalidate an unpopular government power, it tosses the issue back into the public arena. The opponents of a broad interpretation of 'public power' now know that the Court will not give them the victory they seek. They will have to roll up their sleeves and fight the battle in Congress and the state legislatures- where they may well prevail."[118] I find Judge Posner's take on this case a little troubling. Shall we call a "pragmatic" decision like *Kelo* a "Freak-out Decision" as in: "This will really cause everybody to freak out and will be good for the democratic process in the long run."?

Private Contracts

A major hurdle for developing nations, and an obstacle that they have faced historically, are poorly written constitutions – if they have one at all – and weak judicial systems. For an economy to thrive, the participants in that economy must know that when they enter a contract it will be enforced by the law. Without the possibility of enforcement, either party is free to ignore the contract and breach it with impunity. Whether by corruption or a weak body of law, if a contract doesn't have enforceability, teeth, if you will, economic participants are left to rely on good will or luck. The problem with good will, as any lawyer knows, is that two honest, well meaning parties can have a dispute, not because of venality, but because each has a different recollection of the duties under the contract. That's why lawyers love written contracts, and that's why everybody should love them. It makes everything easier and more predictable – and it helps to avoid disputes. But if there is no enforcement, you're at risk. Another problem is a system of government that doesn't respect the legitimacy of private contracts. If a Hugo Chavez can simply nullify your contractual relations, you are unlikely to want to invest in Venezuela, and risk losing your investment at the whim of the strongman. For an economic system to work, the government must treat private contracts as inviolable – unless the Supreme Court comes up with a reason to set aside the contract. Uh oh. Here comes the Fed. In the immortal words of President Ronald Reagan: The nine most terrifying words in the English language are: 'I'm from the government, and I'm here to help.'" So you come to an agreement, you cut a deal, you sign a contract. So what, the government is here to help with this messy stuff, no matter what the Constitution says.

"No state …shall pass…any law impairing the Obligation of Contracts…" US Constitution Article I, Section 10. Like the Commerce Clause, this appears to be clear and unambiguous. But the Supreme Court did allow a legislature to do just that – impair a private contract. In the 1933 case *Home Building & Loan Association v. Blaisdell*,[119] the court upheld a Minnesota law that prevented properties from being foreclosed even if the mortgagee was in default. The purpose of the law was to protect property owners from foreclosure during the Great Depression. The majority opinion discussed the emergency circumstances that would allow for the legislation, despite the words of the constitution. A year later the court decided three companion cases that would become known as the *Gold Standard Cases*.[120] These cases concerned the New Deal legislation in 1933 that simply cancelled, in all contracts, a thing called a "gold clause." A gold clause was commonly used at the time in real estate contracts instead of a cost-of-living escalator. Congress wanted to protect the price of gold because of the depression. The clause provided that a lessor of property could demand to be paid in gold. Instead of providing that another currency could be used, the administration simply invalidated all gold clauses. Thus, a long-term lease would provide for no inflation protection. Dissenting, Justice McReynolds said: "…this is Nero at his worst. The Constitution is gone."[121]

The legislative cancelling of gold clauses in private contracts had more than a theoretical impact. One investor owned a 14-story 143,000 square foot office building in a prime location in a large city in 1931. He signed a long term lease with an insurance company, which included a gold clause as an inflation hedge. Because the gold clauses were wiped out, retroactively, in 1933, the insurance company paid $23,000 per year until 1993, when the then owner was able to get legislative relief. The 1933 value of rentable space was about 20 cents per square foot. In 1993 it was about $14 per square foot, or a commercial rental value of over 20 Million dollars per year.[122]

With the bizarre interpretations of the Commerce Clause, and the almost non-existence of the Contracts Clause, making rational business decisions in the United States has become a challenge.

In the next chapter, I examine the cases that take up most of the dockets in the modern American courts – torts and personal injury cases.

CHAPTER 12

The Wild World of Torts –
America's Most Common Lawsuit.

A tort is a civil wrong, and it may also be a crime. A punch in the nose is the tort of battery, and may also be the crime of battery. Intentional torts are those actions that a *tortfeasor* actually intended to inflict. Intentional torts include: assault; battery; conversion (wrongfully taking someone's property); defamation of character (slander, a spoken defamation and libel, a written defamation.); false imprisonment; trespass; intentional infliction of emotional distress; fraud; and invasion of privacy. A negligent tort is one committed without intent.

Tort cases, most of which are personal injury cases, are the largest part of our court system's dockets. According to the Bureau of Justice Statistics of the Department of Justice, about 60% of state court civil cases are torts, including automobile accidents, medical malpractice and product liability.[123] If tort cases were fuel, the legal system would run on them. In addition to state court cases, torts are also prevalent in the federal courts, including cases arising under federal law and diversity of citizenship cases. As I discussed in Chapter 3, a case where a federal court has jurisdiction because the parties are from different states is one based on *diversity of citizenship*, which means that a simple motor vehicle accident case can be brought in federal court. Tort cases present the system with an endless rainbow of different facts, as diverse as the facts in two different car accidents.

A few years ago, while driving from Santa Fe to Albuquerque, New Mexico, I came upon one of the most amazing advertising road signs I had ever seen. Projecting from the sign was the rear end of a full-sized Buick, and was artfully designed to look as if it had crashed into the sign. In large letters the passing motorist is advised: "Had an accident? Call..." Who said pain can't be fun – and profitable?

What is Personal Injury Law?

Personal injury (PI) law is a subset of tort law, a civil wrong. Usually it's based on negligence, but not always. If you punch me in the nose you have committed the tort of battery, which is an intentional tort, not negligence. But negligence is where the pay dirt is, because negligence means insurance, and a deep pocket. This is because you cannot buy insurance to cover you against intentional acts, which makes a lot of sense. No company is going to insure you for punching people, because you can control that. Insurance is meant to cover you for mistakes, for negligence. That is why a smart lawyer will always allege at least one count of negligence, even if the tort seems to be obviously intentional. The simple allegation of negligence in a lawsuit creates a duty on the part of an insurance company to defend you, and although the company can refuse to pay (indemnify) you if a jury finds no negligence, the very presence of the insurance company will lead to settlement discussions. Getting back to the punch-in-the-nose example, a diligent tort lawyer needs only allege in the complaint that the defendant "carelessly punched plaintiff in the nose." It's at least arguable that the assailant only meant to scare the plaintiff and negligently misjudged his swing, resulting in a broken nose. You're in good hands with Allstate!

Typical personal injury cases include car accidents, slips and falls on someone's property, medical malpractice, or product liability (an injury caused by a defective product or one that failed to warn of its dangers). Police misconduct, including allegations of brutality are an increasingly active area of tort law. PI cases run the gamut of the ways in which someone can get injured. There are also special statutes that confer liability where the normal operation of law would say otherwise. Workers Compensation, which is not a part of personal injury law, is a statutory scheme that protects workers who are injured without regard to fault on the part of the employer. The only requirement is that the injury be work related. The compensation is strictly limited according to preset formulas. A person with a workers compensation claim may also have a separate personal injury claim against a third party, not his employer. For example, a worker injured on the job because of an alleged defect in a drill he was using has a workers compensation claim against his employer, but also has a possible suit against the manufacturer of the drill for product liability. An interesting twist in this scenario is that the drill manufacturer then has the ability to sue the employer and argue that the employer's negligence was a cause of the accident. Lawyers call this being "third partied in." So even though the workers compensation law protects the employer from a direct suit by an employee, the employer can wind up in the case as if it had been directly sued. Beyond workers compensation, there are statutes that do enable an employee to directly sue his employer. The Federal Employers Liability Act (FELA) is for railroad workers, and enables a railroad worker to sue the railroad for "failure top provide a safe place to work." This doesn't even require that the plaintiff prove negligence, only the failure to provide a safe workplace, which might mean something as simple as the employer's allowing an oily floor to exist. The Jones Act, which is for seaman, is the maritime equivalent of the FELA, and allows for liability if the plaintiff proves that a vessel was "unseaworthy," and the oily floor (deck) example is the same.

A wrongful death lawsuit is a type of personal injury case, and can be broken down into two components: the wrongful death case itself, which is brought by the decedents' survivors for the economic loss they suffered as a result of the death; and the *survival action*, which is the claim that could have been made by the decedent before death – that is, the pre-death pain and suffering that decedent may have suffered as a result of the accident. A claim for *pre-impact terror,* or *fear of impending doom* is common in a survival action in a wrongful death case. It is the momentary terror one experiences just before impact. The economic value of a wrongful death lawsuit depends on the financial position of the decedent, just as in a regular personal injury case, The death of a young child, however tragic, does not have much value because the child contributed nothing to the support of his heirs. The only serious economic value in the case of the death of an infant is the survival action for pre-death pain and suffering.

Class Action Lawsuits

Class Action law is a business, plain and simple. If you own any common stock, you will find in your mailbox every week a notice, advising you that you may be a member of a class of people that have a claim against a defendant, usually a very large corporation – the one you own stock in or do business with. You may also be notified because the lawyers handling the suit demanded customer lists from the defendant, such as your utility company, an insurance company, or your cable tv provider, and you're on the list. The idea is simple. Some matters are just too small for a single person to sue somebody over, and if a company has been screwing its thousands of customers out of a few bucks a year, and you put all of those customers together into a lawsuit, well, now we're talking business – *Big Business*. Legislators wrote the laws enabling such suits on the theory that the law firms bringing the case would be acting as *private attorneys general*. So injustices get corrected without cost to the taxpayer, without individuals having to put up a fee, and the evil big corporation gets its ass handed to it. Recall that in Chapter 1 I discussed a class action lawsuit against Allstate and Farmers Insurance Companies over a practice called "double rounding." Under this method an insurer would "round up' a premium of, say, $1,000.50 to $1,001. The companies would then round again for semi-annual premiums. So $500.50 becomes $501, resulting in a driver paying $1,002 annually, or an extra $1.50 per year. The case settled. Each plaintiff-driver in the class got $5.50 (yes, five dollars and fifty cents), and the attorneys received a fee of $10.3 Million. So class action lawsuits are definitely a big business, and you and I are the products on the shelf. I don't know about you, but I couldn't care less, had I been one of the plaintiffs in the suit against Allstate and Farmers, about the lousy $5.50 reward that was won for me. Hardly worth the time to fill out the paperwork. But so what. I'm the product on the shelf, not an aggrieved plaintiff in a normal lawsuit, and the attorneys care as much about me as I care about the $5.50. So the class action law firms, as part of their business, research all the little bitty nasties that sometimes happen to a lot of people, and multiply those little bitties into big buckies. They then point the shotgun full of the bits of evidence and insert it into the ribs of the evil corporation. The Supreme Court finally got fed up with this nonsense, and recently decided a case that brings some rationality to the game. In April, 2011 the high court said that under the Federal Arbitration Act companies can force disgruntled customers to arbitrate their complaints as individuals, not as part of a group, if there was an arbitration clause in their contract.[124] Because there is an arbitration clause in virtually every contract you sign with a large company, this case may be the end of class action lawsuits as we have known them.

Getting Clients

Ever since lawyers were allowed to advertise their ser-vices,[125] personal injury lawyers have created an artistic genre of ways to round up clients. On radio, TV, and in all sorts of printed material, we are encouraged to call an 800 number because a "cash award may be waiting for you." One of my personal favorites is a New York guy who tells you how great he is while in the background there is a voice-over reciting every possible bit of may-hem that might befall a human being. I'm paraphras-ing, but it goes something like: "If you have suffered a slipped disc, herniated disc, fracture, slip and fall, medical malpractice, a defective product, brain injury, food poisoning..." You get the idea. From a marketing viewpoint it's a great ad. The listener may have not have thought in terms of a lawsuit, but one of the magic words registers, and the result is a phone call, which is the purpose of the ad. A listener, having recently suffered a bout of Salmonella, hears the words "food poisoning" followed by "large cash award," and he's fumbling for his cell phone.

Corporate or real estate lawyers get business by good old fashioned networking, and also by reputation. A person buying or selling real estate would usually ask the real estate broker or a friend who they would suggest as a lawyer. A corporate attorney gets business from the networking and ongoing practices of the business of business. But for a personal injury lawyer, there is a problem. Accident victims are not members of a normal network, and we hope, the accident is a one-time or at least rare occurrence. There is no club you can join where the members have all had recent accidents. There are also shady ways of getting personal injury business, most of which are illegal. The term *ambulance chaser* refers to the practice of finding an accident victim shortly after an accident, the most opportune time. Some lawyers would actually monitor the emergency frequencies, appear at the scene of an accident, and literally follow the ambulance to the hospital. At the hospital, assuming the victim was accessible, the lawyer would stop by to say hello, saying that he was down the hall visiting another client and heard of the victim's plight. Some unscrupulous practitioners would also arrange for friendly nurses or other medical professionals to let them know when an accident victim appeared. In a scene from the movie *The Verdict,* Paul Newman appeared at a wake (for a person he didn't know) and, expressing his sympathies to the family, handed them his business card. Ambulance (or hearse) chasing is illegal in all states, as is providing a finder's fee to a third party who tipped the attorney off.

A legitimate, and probably the best way for plaintiff personal injury lawyers to get clients, is to establish relationships with other attorneys who don't practice personal injury law. The referring lawyer gets paid a fee by the PI lawyer, usually a percentage of the PI lawyer's fee. This is perfectly legitimate, because the parson making the referral is an attorney, and attorneys are allowed to split fees. This is similar to the English arrangement, where a solicitor (a lawyer who does not try cases in a courtroom) brings a case to a barrister (trial lawyer). This generally works to everyone's advantage. The referring attorney won't just send cases to a trial lawyer because he's an old crony. To get the best result for his client, and himself, he is motivated to send the case to a very experienced and talented PI lawyer. The client also has the advantage of an intermediary to complain to if there is a problem. Because the PI lawyer wants to keep on good terms with the referring attorney in hopes of getting future referrals, he will make it his business to see that the referring attorney's client gets treated properly

Damages

Justice demands that all people are treated equally before the law. In a personal injury lawsuit, however, equal treatment depends on where you start and how much your losses are, which depends a great deal on your economic position when you were injured. There are two parts to the damages issue in a personal injury suit:

economic damages and non-economic damages. Economic damages, as the name implies, means those damages that you suffer from a strictly economic or financial perspective, and it is one that is personal to the injured plaintiff. In tallying up the economic damages the attorney, often with the help of a forensic economist, will look to all that you have lost because of the accident. The major part of these losses include medical bills and lost wages, including lost or reduced pension benefits. If two people of similar age and health are injured in separate accidents, the plaintiff with the higher income will be entitled to more in economic damages. The logic of this is inescapable. The lost income of an investment banker, for example, will be much higher than that of a postal clerk. It's difficult to argue that there is any injustice here: You should be able to recover what you lost, and no more. The accident took away part of your income; the law says that it should be compensated for.

Non-economic damages includes such things as your pain and suffering, and can also include compensation for emotional damages, loss of the enjoyment of life, as well as the loss of sexual intimacy with a spouse, who may also have a separate claim for this item of damages. All together these kinds of damages are known as *hedonic damages*. In the hands of a skilled trial lawyer, these damages provide a broad brush with which to paint a picture for the jury. The jury must consider the following questions: What is the value of pain that, according to medical testimony, will last the rest of your life? What is the value of the loss of your spouse's sexual intimacy for the rest of your life? What is the value of the emotional pain for a professional musician who has been rendered deaf by an accident? The answer to these questions is not a simple formula. It is strictly prohibited to give jurors guidelines, such as past verdicts for similar injuries – although such information is often used in settlement negotiations. It is a question of helping the jury to come up with numbers based on impassioned words. This is where a skilled trial lawyer earns his fee, quite literally because it is usually a fee contingent on the outcome.

The Contingent Fee

In a PI lawsuit, the lawyer is typically paid a contingent fee, meaning that the fee is contingent on a settlement or judgment resulting from a jury verdict, and the fee is generally one-third of the net proceeds of the case. This is what those ads mean when you hear a voice saying "free consultation," "No fee unless we get you money" or "The advice is free." Think of it as a commission based on the sale of a product, the product being your case, and the buyer the jury.

The contingent fee is a rallying point for tort reformers, who argue that, because the plaintiff has no financial risk if he loses, he has an incentive to sue. Rather, the reformers argue, an injured plaintiff should hire a lawyer and pay the fee regardless of the outcome. In the United States, the fee is purely contingent, and is very much like a commission to a salesman – a percentage of the award. Until quite recently, the United States was the only legal system to allow contingent fees. As of 2004, there were only ten or so countries with contingent fees.[126] In England it is known as a *conditional* fee, meaning no success – no fee. But there is a big difference between the English conditional fee and the American contingent fee. In England, the barrister is required to keep his billing sheets just as any lawyer, writing down in a log all of the time he spent on the case. If the case is successful, the barrister gets paid, but no more than 100% of the normal hourly billing as calculated from the billing sheets. In the U.S. a lawyer can strike gold with a large case. With a typical one-third contingent fee, a $30 million verdict will result in a fee of $10 million. Even if the lawyer's hourly fee was $500 per hour, he would have to put in over 20,000 hours on your case alone to hit that number. There is very big money in contingent fee cases.

The contrary argument in favor of contingent fee cases is that it opens the courtroom door to people who could not possibly afford to pay the legal fees in a lawsuit. This is obviously true. It can take tens of thousands of dollars in expenses alone to mount a complicated case such as a product liability lawsuit. If an injured plaintiff is a store clerk making $19,000 per year his options for justice shrink to zero. Any plaintiff's lawyer will also point out that the lawyer takes all of the risk in a contingent fee case. This is also true, but the risks are lessened if the lawyer does his homework carefully before taking a case to make sure that the case has a shot at success. Many lawyers will take a case where the liability situation is doubtful, but the injury is catastrophic, and therefore worth the risk. Some prominent and successful PI attorneys will take such cases often, knowing that their reputation alone will get the defense to put money on the table. The defense lawyer may have come to the conclusion that his client didn't cause the accident, but the plaintiff is a quadriplegic, and all of the evidence on damages tells a tragic and sad story. Does he risk a multimillion dollar award from a teary eyed jury against his client – or does he put an offer on the table?

The reputation of a PI attorney can have a gigantic impact on the value of a case. When I published *The New York Jury Verdict Reporter* I had a strict policy of sending a copy of the published report to the attorneys that I interviewed. One prominent PI lawyer in Manhattan would frame and hang each report in his waiting room. He called it his "wailing wall." The purpose was to show clients that they were in the right place, and also to show defense lawyers, while waiting to conference a case with him, that they had a bear to grapple with. In any field of the law, a big reputation will make a big impression on the opposition. Imagine you are sitting across the table from a David Boies, a Jerry Spence, or an F. Lee Bailey. You will pay very careful attention.

The Attorney Recommends, the Client Decides

In the movie *A Civil Action*, John Travolta plays the lead lawyer in a big and complicated environmental lawsuit. He makes the mistake a lot of lawyers make: he falls in love with his case, and goes broke bringing it to trial. In the famous scene where the defense attorney, played by Robert Duval, shoves a piece of paper to Travolta while they are sitting in the hallway during a break in trial. The paper had a large number written on it, clearly indicating a settlement offer. Travolta's character doesn't communicate the offer to the clients. This is wrong, although the silver screen sometimes stretches facts for dramatic effect. Any offer, no matter how insignificant, must be communicated to the client. The attorney can urge that the client refuse the offer, but ethics requires the lawyer to communicate it to the client.

Who is at fault? Contributory and Comparative Negligence

The doctrine of contributory negligence holds that if a plaintiff is guilty of any negligence at all in causing the accident that injured him, there will be no money awarded. A veteran tort defense lawyer I knew loved to instill some drama into a case. He would always sum up to a jury by tearing off a tiny piece of paper from a page, and say: "Do you find the plaintiff was guilty of this much negligence?" If the jury so found, the plaintiff would not receive a nickel. That was when New York was a "strict" contributory negligence state.

Strict contributory negligence is a harsh rule, and only a few states still follow it. Most states have adopted *comparative negligence*, a doctrine that allows for recovery even if plaintiff contributed to the accident, and the recovery is reduced by his percentage fault. A variation is the 50% Rule, which bars recovery if plaintiff is more than 50% at fault. A typical jury sheet has the following questions:

1. Do you find the defendant negligent?

2. If the answer to question 1 is yes, what percentage fault do you find against defendant?

3. Do you find the plaintiff negligent?

4. If the answer to question 3 is yes, what percentage fault do you find against plaintiff?

If the answer to question 4 is 51% in a state that follows the 50% Rule, plaintiff collects nothing.

Open those Deep Pockets – The Joint and Several Liability Doctrine

Plaintiff was pushing her infant son in a stroller, with her toddler daughter next to her, across a very busy intersection in Manhattan. She was crossing in front of a large tractor trailer truck, the kind with the long straight engine hood. The light changed, and the truck driver, not seeing her because of his limited sight distance over the large engine hood, moved forward, crushing and killing her infant son, and severely injuring her and her daughter, both physically and psychologically. In the ensuing lawsuit, plaintiff claimed that the driver was negligent because he should not have proceeded unless he knew there was nobody in front of him; that the truck manufacturer was negligent because there should have been in place mirrors to counteract the limited line of sight; and that the City of New York was negligent because the green/red light interval was not long enough. The jury found the truck driver 40% negligent, the manufacturer (which happened to be in bankruptcy at the time) 59% liable, and finally, the City of New York was found 1% negligent based on the timing of the light. The jury returned a verdict of over $20 million. The truck driver had the minimal required insurance, the manufacturer, in bankruptcy, had its required minimum. Jurors were surprised to hear after the verdict that the City of New York (one Percent liable) was on the hook for almost the entire award.[127] This is the impact of the doctrine of "joint and several liability," also known as the *deep pockets doctrine*, and is the law in the vast majority of states. It is known as the deep pockets doctrine because it enables a plaintiff's attorney to find a defendant who can pay the entire sum of a jury award, just by convincing the jury that the deep pocket party is in any percentage responsible for the negligence. The jury in the above hypothetical made their decision, thinking that the City of New York was on the hook for only two hundred thousand dollars, not the substantial part of $20 million. It is not uncommon for a jury to feel that they have been hoodwinked in a case like this. In any lawsuit where plaintiff's attorney has determined that there are very few financially responsible parties from whom to collect a judgment, the hunt is on for any party with deep pockets whom a jury might find one percent liable. When I learned this is law school, I felt it was unjust. I asked my torts professor after class why, in his opinion, such a doctrine should exist. His response: "Why should a plaintiff be required to find out who to collect from?" My follow up question was going to be: "Well why not?" I didn't ask it. Never pick an argument with a law professor.

No-Fault Insurance

Some states have a type of automobile insurance known as no-fault coverage. With a no-fault policy you collect damages from an accident without regard to fault, but the amount that you can collect is very limited, and aims to provide compensation for medical expenses and lost wages, but not pain and suffering. In some states it is mandatory, in others it is your choice. What you give up with no-fault insurance is the ability to sue another driver in court – you are stuck with the coverage limits. In New York, for example, you are covered for up to $50,000, regardless of fault, for basic economic loss (medical expenses, lost wages, and certain other limited expenses). But you can still sue if you have suffered a "serious injury." The statute tries its best to define just what a serious injury is, but a lot is left to litigate. The New York No-Fault law defines a serious injury as one: that results in death; dismemberment; a significant disfigurement; a fracture; the loss of a fetus; permanent loss of use of a body organ, member, function or system; permanent consequential limitation of use of a body organ or member; significant limitation of use of a body function or system; or a medically determined injury or impairment of a non- permanent nature which prevents the injured person from performing substantially all of the material acts which constitute such person's usual and customary daily activities for not less than 90 days during the 180 days immediately following the occurrence of the injury or impairment". Just as with any statute that tries to clearly define a possibly vague subject, the New York No-Fault law is a perfect example of an attempt to simplify, but results in more confusion. Say, for example, you fracture a finger. Voila, according to the simple words of the statute, you're in, and you can sue in court. But if, on the other hand, you suffer a scar across your nose, the question becomes, is this a "significant disfigurement" as required by the statute. Whether it is "significant" will have to be determined by a separate legal proceeding before the lawsuit can go forward. It's easy to pick on the legislature, but, when defining rights, the lawmakers are limited to the use of language, a form of communication that is not always precise.

Medical Malpractice

A lawsuit that claims that a doctor or hospital was negligent is a *medical malpractice suit*. The complaint alleges that a treatment fell below the *standard of care* that is legally expected of a medical professional. The only way that a breach of the standard of care can be proven, or even submitted to the jury, is through the testimony of an expert witness, who has the expertise to give an *opinion* that the incident fell below the standard. For the expert to take the stand there must either be a stipulation by the other side that he is indeed an expert on the subject, or he must submit to *voir dire* (detailed questioning before the judge). It is then up to the judge to determine if the expert can testify. For example, a case involving negligent childbirth would require the testimony of an obstetrician/gynecologist. An orthopedic surgeon would not qualify because the matter is beyond her particular expertise. Without an expert, you can't even get to trial. A scene from the otherwise excellent movie *The Verdict* annoyed a lot of lawyers, me included. The movie was about a medical malpractice case. At a key dramatic moment, Paul Newman's character excitedly shouts to his assistant: "I have an expert witness!" No kidding Paul – no expert, no case. Some movies are more fun if you're not a lawyer.

Medical malpractice is front-and-center in the ongoing debate over health care in America. Reformers argue that fear of a malpractice lawsuit forces physicians to practice defensive medicine, ordering test upon test, lest they be confronted on the witness stand for failing to order a certain diagnostic process. There is also a battle cry, which has taken on a life of its own, that the nation's medical malpractice litigation is bogged down

by frivolous lawsuits. There is a general belief that baseless claims clog the system and force out more serious
ones. But to accept the idea that there is a prolifera-
tion of frivolous medical malpractice lawsuits, one has
to accept the correlative idea that the nation is clogged
with stupid lawyers. You may not like lawyers, or even
respect them, but that doesn't matter. What does matter is that, although their intelligence varies as in any
group, the universe of medical malpractice plaintiff lawyers does not consist of people who want to waste time
and lose money. The point is that a medical malpractice
lawsuit is a complex operation, requiring a vast amount
of investigation, study, analysis, and consultation with
expert witnesses. The fee, almost universally, is a contingent one, so the attorney fronts all of the costs to evaluate the case. Because of this, the plaintiff's lawyer can
simply not afford to take a case that has little chance of
success. Research bears this out. The Harvard School
of Public Health did a study of 1,452 closed claims over
five different insurance companies across the country.
The results, published in the prestigious New England
Journal of Medicine, cast serious doubt on the idea that
frivolous claims are rife. Most claims (72%) that did
not involve error did not receive compensation. When
they did, the payments were lower, on average, than
payments for claims that did involve error ($313,205
vs. $521,560). Among claims that involved error, 73%
received compensation. "Overall, the malpractice system appears to be getting it right about three quarters
of the time," said David Studdert, professor of law and
public health at Harvard and one of the lead authors of
the study. "That's far from a perfect record, but it's not
bad, especially considering that questions of error and
negligence can be complex." The 27% of cases with

outcomes that didn't match their merit included claims that went unpaid even though the injury was caused by an error (16%); claims that were paid but did not involve error (10%); and claims that were paid but did not appear to involve a treatment-related injury (0.4%).[128] The study did not praise the current system, but only pointed out the above results, which contest the notion that the claims are out of control. But the study also found that the costs of the current medical malpractice litigation system is quite high. Administrative costs, including legal fees, amount to 54% of the amount eventually paid out in compensation.

The current system of compensation for medical malpractice is not without problems, and the cost per claim is high, but it is clear that "fixing" the system is not a silver bullet for solving health care costs in the country.

But what statistics don't show is the toll that the system takes on the individual physician. When an attorney has determined that there is a viable case, the next step is to decide just who may be at fault: the attending physician, the doctor making night rounds, the radiologist, the anesthesiologist, who? The cautious response is to "sue everybody in sight," and let the facts sort themselves out during the discovery process. It's hard to fault the lawyer for this strategy, but the result can be endless rounds of depositions, not to mention the Sword of Damocles hovering over a doctor's head during the litigation. And the problem is especially felt among primary care physicians in private practice. The *New York Times* recently carried an article about a family physician who tried to sell his practice, and, after getting no offers, decided to give it away – still no results! The share of solo practices among members of the

American Academy of Family Physicians fell to 18 % by 2008 from 44 % in 1986. And census figures show that in 2007, just 28 % of doctors described themselves as self-employed, compared with 58% in 1970.[129] These numbers are not solely caused by high medical malpractice premiums, but in a practice that becomes increasingly burdened by paperwork and costs, the huge premiums are not a help.

Product Liability

In a lawsuit based on *product liability*, the plaintiff must prove that the product that caused the injury was either *defective*, or that there was a *failure to warn*, or both. As in a medical malpractice case, expert testimony is needed to prove the allegations, unless the defect was so obvious that a juror could come to a decision based on his own life experience, which is extremely rare. A product may be completely free of defects, yet defendant can be liable if there was a failure to warn the user of a danger. This has led to a cottage industry of warnings on just about any product we use. There is an organization called the Michigan Lawsuit Abuse Watch (mlaw.org) that holds an ongoing contest for what it calls Wacky Warning Labels. Some of the stranger entries include:

- A label on a baby stroller warns: "Remove child before folding"

- A fishing lure with a three-pronged hook warns: "Harmful if swallowed"

- A popular scooter for children warns: "This product moves when used."

- A nine- by three-inch bag of air used as packing material cautions: "Do not use this product as a toy, pillow, or flotation device."

- A flushable toilet brush warns: "Do not use for personal hygiene."

- A label on an electric hand blender warns: "Never remove food or other items from the blades while the product is operating."

- A digital thermometer that can be used to take a person's temperature several different ways warns: "Once used rectally, the thermometer should not be used orally."

- A household iron warns users: "Never iron clothes while they are being worn"

- A label on a hair dryer reads, "Never use hair dryer while sleeping"

- A warning on an electric drill made for carpenters cautions: "This product not intended for use as a dental drill."

- A label on a bottle of drain cleaner warns: "If you do not understand, or cannot read, all directions, cautions and warnings, do not use this product."

But product liability lawsuits are a serious matter, and the strange warning labels we see are the everyday reminders that something big is going on. In 1980 there were 4,792 product liability cases in the Federal Courts out of a total of 29,420 tort suits of all kinds. By 2003, the number of product liability cases had increased to 27,402 out of a total of 49,166 tort cases. So in 1980, product liability cases were 16% of the total; in 2003, 56%.[130]

The idea behind the tort of product liability is simple: if a company puts a product out there for us to buy, the product should be safe. In the catacombs of federal agencies, many are addressed to the safety of products, most significantly, the Consumer Product Safety Commission, the Food and Drug Administration, and the Agriculture Department. The tort system is another regulatory regime, that works through private lawsuits rather than regulation.

You cannot turn on the TV without being bombarded with ads looking for plaintiffs that have been injured by various products. Asbestos exposure, and a resulting disease, mesothelioma, are probably the most common. Hundreds of thousands of Americans worked in industries that used asbestos over the years. What was once called the "miracle mineral," asbestos is now known to cause devastating illness if inhaled over time in its dry form floating in the air (friable). There are law firms that specialize in, and do little else than litigate, asbestos claims. Besides the asbestos ads, there are countless ads concerning medications that have been found to cause serious complications. Probably the most notorious medication is Thalidomide, a sedative introduced in the 1950s, but was later withdrawn when it was found to cause devastating birth defects.

Reformers argue that product liability claims stifle innovation, and keep good products off the shelves because the would-be manufacturers fear lawsuits, and that frivolous claims create a drag on the economy. But proving that there is an innovation problem as a result of litigation fear is almost impossible, because you are trying to prove a reason why something hasn't happened. Nobody can argue that frivolous lawsuits are a bad thing, but, just as I discussed with medical malpractice cases, no law firm is going to invest its fortunes in a case that is unlikely to succeed. Just as with medical malpractice, product liability suits are expensive. It is also difficult, if not impossible, to determine how many product claims are truly frivolous, because frivolity is in the eyes of the beholder. Consider the famous, or infamous, McDonald's hot coffee case.

The Poster Child of Product Liability Frivolity – Was it Really Frivolous?

The McDonald's "hot coffee case" has entered the realm of American legend. How can a woman sue and be awarded millions for being burned when she put a coffee cup between her legs? Frivolous? Lets look at the facts. 79 year-old Ms. Liebeck was a front seat passenger in a car driven by her nephew. After they bought coffee at a McDonald's drive-through, the nephew pulled the car over to a parking area so his aunt could put cream and sugar into the coffee. NOTE – the car was not moving. Ms. Liebeck steadied the coffee between her knees and attempted to pull the top off, spilling the entire cup onto her lap. She suffered *third degree burns* to her thighs, buttocks and groin. Because she was wearing cotton pants, the fabric held the hot liquid against her body. She was hospitalized for 8 days, underwent skin grafting, and lost 20 pounds. She required 2 years of follow-up medical care. Her attorney argued, not that it was negligent to serve hot coffee, but that it was *unreasonably dangerous* to serve coffee *that* hot. A 12-member jury awarded her $200,000 in compensatory damages (which was reduced to $160,000 because they also found that she was 20% comparatively negligent), and $2.7million in punitive damages. The trial judge reduced the punitive damages to $480,000 – three times the compensatory damages, for a total judgment of $640,000. Newspapers screamed and the nation freaked out. Hold it right there. Why did everybody go crazy over the verdict? The answer is simple. A quick summary of the facts seemed to indicate that something was amiss. Woman buys hot coffee, puts it between her legs, gets burned and blames somebody else. Case closed, in the court of public opinion. But nothing can pour cold water (pardon the pun) on a hot story faster than looking at the facts. The evidence showed that the coffee was served at 180° F, and expert testimony proved that such heat can produce third degree burns in about 12 seconds, not enough time to pull off garments or take other steps to stop the burning. The evidence also showed that McDonald's had over 700 complaints of excessively hot coffee in the 10 years before the incident. The case settled for an undisclosed amount while on appeal. The case still generates controversy, some arguing that it shows a tort system out of control, while others see it as a rather routine application of facts and law. You be the judge.

Excessive Jury Verdicts – How Much is too Much? What is Just?

To appreciate the difficulty of a judge's job, look no further than the question of whether a jury verdict was excessive or inadequate. Large jury verdicts grab headlines nationwide, and have become the stuff of tort reformers' angst and editorial writers' prose. The jury, as the finder of fact, determines the monetary award, and then the judge must decide on the numerous post-trial motions. Often it is a motion to set aside the verdict because the award was excessive. The problem for a judge is vexing – How much is too much? Consider, for example, a personal injury case where the defendant was found to be 100% negligent. The plaintiff suffered a fractured tibia or shinbone. The break was mid-shaft, meaning that the knee or ankle was not involved. The fracture is set, and healed without complication. Plaintiff incurred medical and drug expenses and lost a few weeks from her job, resulting in *economic damages* of $65,000, which the jury so found. Then came the question of non-economic damages, primarily pain and suffering, where the creative and persuasive skills of the trial lawyer can result in a damages award sometimes appearing poetic. In this hypothetical, the jury awarded plaintiff $10 million for pain and suffering from her leg fracture. Ridiculous? Most would think so, except for plaintiff and her attorney. The case then goes to the trial judge to decide on defendant's post- trial motion to set aside the verdict as excessive. First, of course, the judge looks to the law. Most states apply a common law standard in determining whether a verdict is excessive, and the standard applied is whether the verdict "shocks the conscience of the court." Ok, let's assume that the judge decides that her conscience has been shocked. How much has it been shocked? Some judges will advise attorneys for both sides that a decision will be handed down by a certain date, and then suggests that they confer with their clients and try to come up with a settlement. This is as it should be. If both sides can come to a mutually agreeable number, the case is closed and the system moves on. Sometimes, however, a settlement is not reached, and it is up to the judge to render a decision. The judge's decision will often be something like the following: "I find that the verdict is against the weight of the evidence and that the amount of $10 million shocks the conscience of the court; I hereby reduce the verdict to $500,000, which, if agreeable to the parties, shall be entered as a judgment, otherwise I enter judgment for a new trial." This clearly puts the heat on both parties – accept the amount or begin the expensive and time-consuming process of appeal. But how did the judge come up with the number of $500,000? There is no clear and objective way of knowing, just as there is no objective way of knowing how the jury came up with $10 million. Most trial lawyers will refer to publications known as "jury verdict reporters" to come up with settlement demands and offers – Full disclosure: I was the founder and publisher for 20 years of *The New York Jury Verdict Reporter*, now known as *Verdictsearch, New York.*. The idea behind such research is to answer the question: "What have past juries awarded for cases involving similar injuries?" But that is no guidance for a judge making a decision on the size of a jury award because those similar verdict reports lack one thing: they are not part of the evidence record before the judge. Some states have abandoned the common law principle of "shocks the conscience" and have tried to be more objective by statute. New York, for example, codified a new standard for determining whether a verdict is excessive. New York judges now look to whether a verdict "deviates materially from what would be reasonable compensation."[131] Well, your honor, that clears it up, doesn't it? What is *reasonable* you may ask, and what is a *material deviation*? With all due respect to the New York State legislature, I cannot criticize this statutory formula, because I can't come up with a better one. The introduction of the word "reasonable" was an obvious attempt on the part of the legislature to try to create a more objective standard, or at least more objective than "shocks the conscience." *Reasonable* is a word strewn throughout the law, as a nod toward intelligence and civility of the person making the determination of what is reasonable. In the investment world there is the reasonable person standard when making decisions where to put a client's money. Throughout leases and commercial agreements there appears the word reasonable. But it is easier stated than applied. It is a statutory attempt, just as the common law tried with "shocks the conscience," to come up with a way of saying: "Hell, that's just too much money," although that's exactly what the common law and the statutes mean. So it is left to judges, both trial and appellate, to come up with a figure that the jury got wrong. Nobody said the job of judging is easy.

What Happens in the Jury Room. My Uncle the Expert Witness.

The sanctity of the jury deliberation room has an almost religious aura in our history. The jurors receive their instructions or "charge" from the judge, explaining their job and the law. They are then on their own, with no official watching over them. If they have a question, they can ask it of the judge, but they are in charge of their own decision on the facts. No words can say it better than the classic movie *Twelve Angry Men*, where Henry Fonda's character persuades the contrary group that they should

carefully sift through the evidence and not jump to a con-
clusion. His efforts resulted in acquitting the criminal
defendant rather than sentencing him to death. The film
is inspiring, and it reminds one of how the American jury
system can work so well. It also reminds me of how the
system can sometimes break down. A dear late uncle
of mine was a delightful guy, but did suffer from being
opinionated – in spite of the facts. Over dinner he told me
excitedly about his recent jury duty on a personal injury
case. The lawsuit involved a woman in a department
store walking down the aisle looking at a rack of dresses.
She testified that she tripped over a raised electrical box
on the floor, causing her to fall and suffer injuries. There
were no eyewitnesses. It was her testimony that the box
protruded a foot or so into the aisle from the platform
holding the dress rack. There was no contrary evidence
to dispute her claim of where the box was placed. The
jury found in favor of the department store, determining
that there was no negligence on its part. "From what you
told me, it seems to me that her story was pretty believ-
able," I said. "Why did you find in favor of the store,
especially because nobody disputed her explanation of
the facts?" Uncle, who prided himself on being a handy
man and well versed in matters technical, was able to
convince his fellow jurors that: "No tradesman could be
so dumb as to leave an electrical box in the middle of the
floor. They always recess them in the platform." When I
explained to uncle that plaintiff's story was *the evidence*,
and not his theory, he again explained that no tradesman
could be so dumb as to leave the box in the middle of
the floor. So uncle and his colleagues made their decision on imaginary facts – not the facts in evidence at the
trial – but the facts as conjured up by uncle and his fellow jurors. Jury deliberations stay in the jury room and

only come out when there is objective reason to suspect jury misbehavior. The judge in that case had nothing to decide: he wasn't aware that new "evidence" was created in the jury room. The poor woman who went splat went home empty-handed, because of uncle's "evidence." I refused to publish that case in *The New York Jury Verdict Reporter.*

Key Elements in the Value of a Personal Injury Lawsuit

A Sympathetic Plaintiff

A plaintiff's personality can have a powerful impact on what a jury will award. I once represented a guy who had a bad fall off a bicycle resulting in some fractured bones and nasty scars. His bike hit a deep rut in a bicycle path in a park. When I put the official in charge of the park on the stand, he testified that he was personally aware of the rut, and had it on a list of things to get around to. A trial lawyers dream! A key witness testified that he had *actual notice* of a defect, a winning piece of evidence. So liability was a lock. On the damages side of the equation, more good news: there was nothing in the pretrial record to dispute the injuries. There was one problem: my client had the sneakiest personality I had ever encountered. In my interviews with him and during pretrial depositions, his whole demeanor said that he was holding something back. Hell – he appeared to be lying! He could not look you in the eye, and when he answered a question he even had a smirk. He was the kind of guy who, if you asked him for the time of day, you would want a second opinion before setting your watch. There was nothing in the evidence so far to contradict the facts of the case – he hit a rut that the park officials were aware of and was severely injured. Who was I, his attorney, to doubt him? This is a judgment call any lawyer has to make in behalf of his client. No way was I going to put mister creepy puss on the witness stand and watch the jury get squirrely eyed and award a minimal verdict. I convinced my client to settle before he took the stand, thereby doing my job. Did I do justice by my client? Did I do the right thing? I never had a doubt about that case.

Credibility of Key Witnesses

A case can die on the spot if the credibility of a crucial witness is impeached. A diligent lawyer will do careful research to see if there is something about the background of a witness can be brought up during testimony. If a doctor's record shows a conviction for fraud, the defense will have a theme to preach to the jury. If the doctor's background shows a history of testifying in personal injury cases, but only for plaintiffs, his credibility is in doubt. And just as in the case of my creepy client, the way the witness testifies will also have a big impact on the jury's ability to believe him. The most dramatic example of credibility bashing occurred during the OJ Simpson trial. The testimony of lead detective Mark Furman was crucial to the prosecution's case. F. Lee. Bailey, whose name is synonymous with diligent lawyering, uncovered audiotapes of Detective Furman speaking to an author who was writing a book on the LA Police Dept., including any issues of race in the department. She asked Furman to describe the tone among detectives concerning race. Voila – The jury heard Furman himself describing the way cops talked about African-Americans, in blunt terms, including the n-word. The articulate detective Furman was reduced to a sputtering wreck.

Where the accident occurred.

As I noted in Chapter 1, the venue (location) of the trial can have a huge impact on a verdict. It is well known among trial lawyers that there are certain counties where juries tend to be very stingy, and some where they will award a pot of gold. All things being equal, a jury in Los Angeles County is likely to render a much larger verdict than in conservative Orange County. A venue of blue collar workers tends to go with the underdog, while wealthier suburbs consist of more green-eyeshade types. This may not seem fair. Neither is life.

Aggravated Liability.

How bad were the actions of the defendant? Was he drunk or driving recklessly? Or was the defendant a nice person who made a simple error in judgment? Can the defense argue on summation: "You heard the testimony of Ms. Defendant. When the police arrived she was not only crying, but she was trying her best to help the plaintiff." Or is there testimony such as this in a case that I worked on – representing the defendant. The evidence showed that defendant was driving in a car with a bunch of other young people. He had cut off the plaintiff motorcyclist, causing him to go off the road, sustaining brain injuries. When the police arrived, according to their testimony, the defendant and friends were standing a few feet from plaintiff, were doing nothing to assist him, and were giggling hysterically. Nice. We lost the case.

How the injury occurred

This is one of the major battle grounds in the debate about capping non-economic damages in medical malpractice cases, and one that I touched on in Chapter 1. Two plaintiffs are injured on the same day. They are the same age, earn the same income and have an identical family life. They both suffer severe spinal injuries, rendering them quadriplegic. Their case is heard in the same county courthouse and by the same jury (hey, this is a hypothetical, roll with it). Liability is uncontested in both cases. One plaintiff was hurt in a car accident and the other by the malpractice of a physician. The state where the trials are heard has a statutory cap of $250,000 on non-economic damages in medical malpractice cases. The car accident victim gets a verdict for pain and suffering of $20 million. The medical malpractice victim gets $250,000. The debate goes on, especially with the new health care reform law. Health care grows increasingly expensive, partially because of what physicians need to charge in order to afford the most expensive part of their overhead – medical malpractice insurance. It is a doctor's job to deal with life and death issues, sometimes making decisions in a split second. Doctors argue that they are being faced with an untenable position. This is not an easy question, and it cannot be answered by any legislator without considering a hypothetical like the one in this paragraph.

The daily drama of tort lawsuits in American courts shows no sign of letting up. There is an entire movement known as Tort Reform, aimed mainly at frivolous lawsuits, but also against the enormous costs to manufacturers, businesses of all types, and the medical profession. Reform ideas are constantly discussed, including damages caps, alternative dispute resolution, a no-fault system for medical malpractice claims, and special courts that handle only medical malpractice cases. Whatever changes occur, if history is any guide, they will be gradual.

Is justice being served by the American tort system?

CHAPTER 13

Conclusion – Is there Justice in America?

A common greeting between old friends goes like this: "How are you doing?" you ask. "Compared to what?" your friend replies. And so it is with Justice in America. How is it? Compared to what? The words of Winston Churchill are repeated often: "Democracy is the worst system in the world, until you consider the alternative." Both Plato and Aristotle believed that the best form of government is a benevolent dictatorship. The benevolent one knows what is good for the people, and is motivated to provide the best justice possible, not for himself, but for his subjects. He is a philosopher-king. As a dictator, he is insulated from the concerns of partisan politics. As a philosopher, he is not motivated by petty concerns, short term popular solutions, feathering his own nest, or even enhancing his legacy. He wants the best for the people, and acts accordingly. Great, if you're a philosopher-king. But last I checked, dictators are plentiful, but benevolent dictators are in short supply. Here's a quiz: Name one.

So what we have is this wonderful mess called American democracy, along with its system of justice. It's easy to be cynical about what goes on, and it's easy to argue that our system is broken. Many of the cases and hypotheticals I discuss in this book could easily lead you to despair. Is that shoplifter really in prison for the next 50 years? People have been wrongfully convicted and sentenced to long prison terms, or even death. Then along comes a scientific breakthrough called DNA testing, and a whole world of wrongs get righted. Before the civil rights movement, an African-American person could not expect the same kind of justice that we all consider our birthright. If you were black, you might as well have lived on a different planet because the things that flowed from American citizenship did not flow to you. But the civil rights movement *did* happen, a nation of people woke up to the wrongs that were meted out because of race, and an entire legal system was reformed, bit by bit, to inject life into the marble-carved saying "Equal Justice Under Law."

There are two great currents flowing through the land that have changed not only our sense of justice, but how justice is delivered. The first current is actually a tsunami, a gigantic wave that is washing over us, and that threatens to drown us: the sense of individual rights as entitlements, and a desire to get those rights down on paper by endless laws, rules, and regulations. John F. Kennedy, in his inaugural address, uttered one of the most quoted quotes ever spoken: "Ask not what your country can do for you. Ask what you can do for your country." Those words, when he spoke them, were not only inspirational, but personal to every listener. They brought tears to our eyes. He spoke to a place in our hearts that wanted to pitch in and help make the nation a better place for all of us, not just for you or me. Today, the words sound quaint, archaic, almost out of place. We have become a nation addicted to asserting our new-found entitlement rights, as if the Constitution was a personal document to enable us get what's coming to us. We once thought of rights as that bundle of guarantees that protected us from the government. We now see our rights as tool kit of instruments that we can use against each other, not to mention the government. We have become so accustomed to our rights, that government at all levels seeks to feed the beast by layers of regulations, and then more layers explaining and amplifying the previous regulations. Leadership and individual responsibility has been supplanted by words on paper, and if those words don't prove sufficient, we add more words and more paper. We have become so paranoid of lawsuits that we clamor for more and more words to help in every situation, because somebody is out there looking to assert a right. A kid breaks a leg? Rip out the jungle gym, or make it so safe with words that it is as exciting as a pillow. We are now seeing regulations on what kids can eat in schools, while the equipment-free playgrounds become useful only for eating twinkies and plunking at hand-held video games.

–The second great current in American justice is the United States Constitution – how it has been turned into something that is barely recognizable. The document itself, through judicial decisions going back to its beginning, has become in many respects a mere historical artifact. When the signers put in a clause giving Congress the power to regulate interstate commerce, they thought that they were doing, well, that. But the interstate commerce clause has been stripped of its plain meaning – to regulate interstate commerce. It is now a clause that feeds power to the central government in a way that was never intended by the framers. The Contracts Clause, found in Article I, Sect 10 of the US Constitution, was also pretty clear: "No state …shall pass…any law impairing the Obligation of Contracts…" If the framers wanted to add a clause immediately after the contracts clause stating "unless the legislature feels otherwise" they would have. The idea of judicial review has become a notion that the courts are a super legislature, an unelected one at that, and if elected representatives got something wrong, the courts will correct the matter.

Do the right thing. How could anybody argue with that? Who could sully the beauty of that simple sentence? When a judge is faced with the plain language of a statute, he will be praised by many that he may have ignored the law in deciding the case, but that's OK because he did the right thing. It is for the legislature to try to do the right thing, and if they get it wrong, the voters will make it right. Doing the right thing is the same as saying, do something with the right intention. I don't have to remind you what paving material is used on the road to hell.

Justice in America is alive and well, but we are in danger of drowning ourselves in law and rules, all in the aim of protecting our new found rights. And by having our constitutional foundation shaken to the core, we find that justice itself is threatened.

This book won't end the debate, but hopefully will keep it going.

Index

Endnotes

[1] www.webster-dictionary.org

[2] Antisocial personality disorder – *Diagnostic and Statistical Manual of Mental Disorders Fourth edition* Text Revision (DSM-IV-TR) American Psychiatric Association (2000) – pages 645–650

[3] John Rawls, *A Theory of Justice*, Harvard University Press, 1971, at p. 60.

[4] *Martinez v. Allstate Insurance Co.*, No. 95-08-09169-CV (Tex. Dist. Ct. Zavala County filed Aug. 28,1995). *Sendejo v. Texas Farmers Insurance Co.*, No. 95-08-09165-CV (Tex. Dist. Ct. Zavala County filed Aug. 30, 1995).

[5] "Rape Victim Stoned to Death in Somalia was 13, U.N. Says," *N.Y. Times*, November 5, 2008, at A12 of the New York Edition

[6] *Lockyer v. Andrade*, 538 US 63 (2003).

[7] Bill Saporito, "How AIG Became Too Big To Fail," *Time*, March 30, 2009, p. 16.

[8] Marcus Luttrell with Patrick Robinson, *Lone Survivor The Eyewitness Account of Operation Redwing and the Lost Heroes of SEAL Team 10*, Little, Brown and Company, 2007, quoted in Michael J. Sandel, *Justice: What's The Right Thing To Do?*, Farrar,Straus and Giroux, 2009, Kindle Edition.

[9] This true story is a summary of a discussion in *Justice: What's The Right Thing To Do?* Id.

[10]   Martha R. Gore, "Waterboarding saved Los Angeles from terrorist attack," examiner.com, April 22, 2009.

[11]   Id.

[12]   I can't find the article, otherwise I would share it with you. Approximately nine zillion articles have been written over the last few years on Credit Default Swaps and other derivative products. It was just the first one that caught my eye. I should have heeded its warning.

[13]   Taleb, Nassim Nicholas), *The Black Swan: The Impact of the Highly Improbable*, Random House, (2007).

[14]   Mike Dash, *Tulipomania The Story of the World's Most Coveted Flower the Extraordinary Passions It Aroused, Crown, 2001.*

[15]   Antonin Scalia, *A Matter of Interpretation*, Princeton University Press (1997) at 13.

[16]   *Marbury v. Madison*, 5 U.S. (1 Cranch) 137 (1803).

[17]   Adam Liptak, "The Case of the Plummeting Supreme Court Docket," *N.Y. Times*, September 29, 2009.

[18]   *Annual Report of the Director: Judicial Business of the United States Courts Table 4.8.*

[19]   Id., at Table 4.9

[20]   American Bar Association, abanet.org, *Statistical Resources.*

21   Common Good, *Returning Sense to American Law*, citing Harris poll, June 27, 2005

22   See, for example Catherine Crier, *The Case Against Lawyers*, Broadway Books, 2002. Ms. Crier, a TV personality and former lawyer and judge, rails against the legal profession, without one citation or note.

23   Carrie Melago, "How Queens school failed Mariya Fatima after stroke." *New York Daily News,* September 10, 2007.

24   Lord Hailsham, *The Door Wherein I Went* (1978) p. 255, quoted in David Pannick, *Judges* ,Oxford University Press at p. 75.

25   Alexander Hamilton, The Federalist No. 78: The Judiciary Department.

26   Bernard Sheintag, *The Personality of the Judge*, (1944) in David O'Brien, *Judges on Judging* , CQ Press, 2009 at p. 80.

27   Philip Kurland, *Of Law and Life and Other Things that Matter*, (1965) p. 75.

28   Felix Frankfurter, The Judicial Process and the Supreme Court, in *Of Law and Men*, Philip Kurland 91956) p. 40.

29   Benjamin Cardozo, The Nature of the Judicial Process, in *Selected Writings of Benjamin Cardozo*, Margaret Hall, (1947) p. 178.

30   *In re J.P. Linehan, Inc.*, 138 F.2d 650, 651-53 (2d Cir. 1943).

31   Richard A. Posner, *How Judges Think*, Harvard University Press, 2008, at p. 81.

32   A. P. Herbert, *Uncommon Law* (1977 edn.) p. 156.

33   National Center for State Courts, www.ncsconline.org/wc/courtopics/FAQs.asp?topic=JudAdm#FAQ1193

34   *Gordon v. Justice Court*, 12 Cal 3d (1974)

35   William Glaberson, "Broken Bench," *New York Times*, September 26, 2006.

36   Id.

37   *Loving v. Virginia*, 388 U.S. 1 (1967)

38   Two Year Update to the Action Plan nycourts.gov/whatsnew/pdf/JusticeCourts2YearUpdate

39   *New York Times*, January 8, 2010.

40   Adam Liptak,, "American Exception – Rendering Justice, with One Eye on Re-election," *New York Times,* May 25, 2008

41   Id. At p. 26.

42   National Center for State Courts

43   American Bar Association, *Fact Sheet on Judicial Selection Methods in the States.*

44   ABA Code of Judicial Conduct, Table of Contents

45   *Caperton et al. v. A. T. Massey Coal co., inc., et al.* No 08-22, June 8, 2009

46   *Tumey v. Ohio*, 273 U. S. 510, 523.

[47]   *Caperton* at p. 28.

[48]   Id at p. 40.

[49]   "The New Politics of Judicial Elections," Brennan Center for Justice at NYU and National Institute on Money in State Politics, published by the Justice at Stake Campaign, February 2002

[50]   Id.

[51]   *New York Times*, October 1, 2006.

[52]   National Center for State Courts, http://www.ncsconline.org/WC/CourTopics/FAQs.asp?topic=JudSel#FAQ633

[53]   Debra Cassens Weiss, "O'Connor: Want a Qualified, Impartial Judiciary? Don't Use Contested Elections," *ABA Journal.com*, December 10, 2009.

[54]   Better Courts for Missouri, http://newmoplan.com/faq

[55]   "Missouri Brakes: The Sue Me State reconsiders judicial elections" *Wall Street Journal* April 18, 2009, p. A12

[56]   Tony Messenger, "Missouri Plan for selecting judges faces new challenge," stltoday.com, November 27, 2010.

[57]   A.G. Sulzberger, "Ouster of Iowa Judges Sends Signal to the Bench," *NY Times*, November 3, 2010.

[58]   *Forbes*, April 21, 1997.

[59]   Peter Drucker, interviewed by Peter Schwartz, wired.com.

[60] US Courts website: http://www.uscourts.gov/judicialcompensation/payfactsheet.html

[61] *The Third Branch*, Newsletter of the Federal Courts, Volume 39 Number 2, February 2007.

[62] Evan Thomas and Pat Wingert, "Why We Can't Get Rid of Failing Teachers," *Newsweek*, March 15, 2010

[63] John Merrow, "It's Time to Debate Teacher Tenure," huffingtonpost.com, December 24, 2010.

[64] Report of the *National Commission on the Public Service,* January 2003, at p. 23.

[65] Id.

[66] Id.

[67] Id., emphasis added.

[68] Id. At p. 32

[69] Id. At 26

[70] American Bar Association, http://www.abanet.org/poladv/priorities/judicial_pay/

[71] Federal Judicial Restoration Act of 2007, S. 1638, 110th Cong., 1st Sess. (2007).

[72] Richard A. Posner, *How Judges Think* at 169, Harvard University Press, 2008.

[73] Paul E. Greengberg and James A. Haley, "The Role of the Compensation Structure in Enhancing Judicial Quality," 15 *Journal of Legal Studies* at 417 (1986) quoted in Posner, Id. at 169.

74   http://www.uscourts.gov/

75   Id.

76   Anthony Lincoln and Robert McEwen, *Lord Eldon's Anecdote Book* (1960) p. 131.

77   Id. At p. 238.

78   Ken Blanchard, *The One Minute Manager*, William Morrow & Company, 1982.

79   Richard Posner, *How Judges Think*, Harvard University Press, 2008 at p. 29.

80   Carol J. Williams, "Supreme Court overturning numerous 9th U.S. Circuit Court of Appeals rulings," *Los Angeles Times*, July 5, 2009.

81   *The Routledge Dictionary of Latin Quotations*, Routledge, New York, 2005.

82   Plato, *The Republic* (transl. H.D.P. Lee, Penguin Classics, 1955), p. 147.

83   http://www.stanford.edu/~dement/apnea.html

84   http://med.stanford.edu/school/Psychiatry/narcolepsy/

85   Ronald R. Grunstein, thesleepclinic.org.uk, "The Case of 'Judge Nodd' and other Sleeping Judges— Media, Society, and Judicial Sleepiness."

86   Bruce Weber, "The Deciders – Umpires v. Judges," *NY Times*, July 11, 2009.

87   New Hampshire Public Radio January 11, 2006 http://www.nhpr.org/node/10177

[88] *Powers v. Harris,* 379 F.3d 1208,(10th Cir. 2004).

[89] U.S. Const. amend. IX.

[90] *Nebbia v. The People of New York State,* 291 U.S. 502 (1934), quoted in Robert A. Levy and William Mellor, *The Dirty Dozen* (Cato Institute 2008) at 188. This work, with a somewhat serendipitous title, is a scholarly exposition of twelve selected Supreme Court cases that have had a disproportionate impact on American law. My analysis of economic cases especially relies on this book.

[91] *Nebbia, 291 U.S.,* at 243-244, McReynolds, J. Dissenting.

[92] *The Dirty Dozen,* Ibid., at 188, citing Timothy Sandefur, "The Right to Earn a Living," Chapman Law Review (2003) at 207.

[93] *United States v. Carolene Products Co.,* 304 U.S. 144 (1938).

[94] *Holmes-Laski Letters: The Correspondence of Mr. Justice Holmes and Harold J. Laski,* vol.2 p. 1124 (Mark DeWolfe Howe. 1953, cited in Richard A. Posner, *How Judges Think,* Harvard University Press, 2008.

[95] *Carolene Products,* 304 U.S. at 155

[96] *Bananas,* United Artists 1971, Woody Allen, Director

[97] Articles of Confederation , Article II

[98] U.S. Const. article 10.

99   *NLRB v. Jones & Loughlin Steel Corp.*, 301 U.S. 1, 37 (emphasis added).

100 *Wickard v. Filburn*, 317 U.S. 111 (1942).

101 Id., at 128-129, quoted in *The Dirty Dozen*, Ibid. at 44.

102 The *Dirty Dozen*, Ibid. at 45.

103 *United States v. Lopez*, 514 U.S. 549 (1995) at 567.

104 *U.S. v. Morrison*, 529 U.S 598 (2000) at 613.

105 Id. quoting U.S. v. Lopez 549 U.S at 564.

106 Id.

107 *Gonzales v. Raich*, 545 U.S. 1 (2005).

108 *Holmes-Laski Letters,* Ibid.

109 *Gonzales*, 545 U.S at 19.

110 *Bananas*, Ibid. at n. x.

111 *Gonzales*, 549 U.S. at 49.

112 Id. At 42.

113 Id. At 47.

114 Health insurance mandate upheld Lyle Denniston, Official reporter for the Supreme Court reporting on the finding that the Individual Mandate is constitutional

115 *Kelo v. City of New London,* 545 U.S. 469 (2005).

116 Id., at 494.

117 Dana Berliner, "Opening the Floodgates: Eminent Domain Abuse in the Post-Kelo World," Institute for Justice, 2006 p. 1, cited in *The Dirty Dozen*, Ibid., at 166.

118 Richard A. Posner, *How Judges Think*, Harvard University Press (2008) at 320..

119 *Home Building & Loan Association v. Blaisdell*, 290 U.S 398 (1934).

120 *Norman v. Baltimore & Ohio Railroad Co.* 294 U.S. 240 (1935*); Nortz v. United States*, 294 U.S. 317 (1935*); and Perry v. United States*, 294 U.S. 330(1935).

121 *Perry*, 294 U.S. at 375, quoted in *The Dirty Dozen*, Id. at 51.

122 *The Dirty Dozen* at p. 50.

123 Department of Justice, Bureau of Justice Statistics," Tort Bench and Jury Trials in State Courts," 2005 http://bjs.ojp.usdoj.gov/content/pub/pdf/tbjtsc05.pdf.

124 *AT&T Mobility, LLC v. CONCEPCION*, No. 09–893.

125 *Bates v. State Bar of Arizona*, 433 US 350 (1977).

126 Herbert M. Kritzer, *Risks, Reputations, and Rewards: Contingency Fee Legal Practice in the United States* (Stanford: Stanford University Press, 2004), 258-259.

127 This hypothetical is adopted from an actual case. I changed the facts a bit to simplify them and to make the hypothetical more understandable.

[128] "Study Casts Doubt on Claims That the Medical Malpractice System Is Plagued By Frivolous Lawsuits," press release, Harvard School of Public Health, May 2006.

[129] "Family Physician Can't Give Away Solo Practice," *New York Times*, April 22, 2011.

[130] Bureau of Justice Statistics, United States Department of Justice, http://bjs.ojp.usdoj.gov/content/glance/tables/tortcldtypetab.cfm

[131] New York Civil Practice Law and Procedure Sect 5501 c (3).

Constitution of the United States of America

We the People of the United States, in Order to form a more perfect Union, establish Justice, insure domestic Tranquility, provide for the common defence, promote the general Welfare, and secure the Blessings of Liberty to ourselves and our Posterity, do ordain and establish this Constitution for the United States of America.

Article I

Section. 1. All legislative Powers herein granted shall be vested in a Congress of the United States, which shall consist of a Senate and House of Representatives.

Section. 2. The House of Representatives shall be composed of Members chosen every second Year by the People of the several States, and the Electors in each State shall have the Qualifications requisite for Electors of the most numerous Branch of the State Legislature.

No Person shall be a Representative who shall not have attained to the Age of twenty five Years, and been seven Years a Citizen of the United States, and who shall not, when elected, be an Inhabitant of that State in which he shall be chosen.

Representatives and direct Taxes shall be apportioned among the several States which may be included within this Union, according to their respective Numbers, which shall be determined by adding to the whole Number of free Persons, including those bound to Service for a Term of Years, and excluding Indians not taxed, three fifths of all other Persons [Modified by Amendment XIV]. The actual Enumeration shall be made within three Years after the first Meeting of the Congress of the United States, and within every subsequent Term of ten Years, in such Manner as they shall by Law direct. The Number of Representatives shall not exceed one for every thirty Thousand, but each State shall have at Least one Representative; and until such enumeration shall be made, the State of New Hampshire shall be entitled to chuse three, Massachusetts eight, Rhode-Island and Providence Plantations one, Connecticut five, New-York six, New Jersey four, Pennsylvania eight, Delaware one, Maryland six, Virginia ten, North Carolina five, South Carolina five, and Georgia three.

When vacancies happen in the Representation from any State, the Executive Authority thereof shall issue Writs of Election to fill such Vacancies.

The House of Representatives shall chuse their Speaker and other Officers; and shall have the sole Power of Impeachment.

Section. 3. The Senate of the United States shall be composed of two Senators from each State, *chosen by the Legislature thereof* [Modified by Amendment XVII], for six Years; and each Senator shall have one Vote.

Immediately after they shall be assembled in Consequence of the first Election, they shall be divided as equally as may be into three Classes. The Seats of the Senators of the first Class shall be vacated at the Expiration of the second Year, of the second Class at the Expiration of the fourth Year, and of the third Class at the Expiration of the sixth Year, so that one third may be chosen every second Year; *and if Vacancies happen by Resignation, or otherwise, during the Recess of the Legislature of any State, the Executive thereof may make temporary Appointments until the next Meeting of the Legislature, which shall then fill such Vacancies* [Modified by Amendment XVII].

No Person shall be a Senator who shall not have attained to the Age of thirty Years, and been nine Years a Citizen of the United States, and who shall not, when elected, be an Inhabitant of that State for which he shall be chosen.

The Vice President of the United States shall be President of the Senate, but shall have no Vote, unless they be equally divided.

The Senate shall chuse their other Officers, and also a President pro tempore, in the Absence of the Vice President, or when he shall exercise the Office of President of the United States.

The Senate shall have the sole Power to try all Impeachments. When sitting for that Purpose, they shall be on Oath or Affirmation. When the President of the United States is tried, the Chief Justice shall preside: And no Person shall be convicted without the Concurrence of two thirds of the Members present.

Judgment in Cases of Impeachment shall not extend further than to removal from Office, and disqualification to hold and enjoy any Office of honor, Trust or Profit under the United States: but the Party convicted shall nevertheless be liable and subject to Indictment, Trial, Judgment and Punishment, according to Law.

Section. 4. The Times, Places and Manner of holding Elections for Senators and Representatives, shall be prescribed in each State by the Legislature thereof; but the

Congress may at any time by Law make or alter such Regulations, except as to the Places of chusing Senators.

The Congress shall assemble at least once in every Year, *and such Meeting shall be on the first Monday in December* [Modified by Amendment XX], unless they shall by Law appoint a different Day.

Section. 5. Each House shall be the Judge of the Elections, Returns and Qualifications of its own Members, and a Majority of each shall constitute a Quorum to do Business; but a smaller Number may adjourn from day to day, and may be authorized to compel the Attendance of absent Members, in such Manner, and under such Penalties as each House may provide.

Each House may determine the Rules of its Proceedings, punish its Members for disorderly Behaviour, and, with the Concurrence of two thirds, expel a Member.

Each House shall keep a Journal of its Proceedings, and from time to time publish the same, excepting such Parts as may in their Judgment require Secrecy; and the Yeas and Nays of the Members of either House on any question shall, at the Desire of one fifth of those Present, be entered on the Journal.

Neither House, during the Session of Congress, shall, without the Consent of the other, adjourn for more than three days, nor to any other Place than that in which the two Houses shall be sitting.

Section. 6. The Senators and Representatives shall receive a Compensation for their Services, to be ascertained by Law, and paid out of the Treasury of the United States. They shall in all Cases, except Treason, Felony and Breach of the Peace, be privileged from Arrest during their Attendance at the Session of their respective Houses, and in going to and returning from the same; and for any Speech or Debate in either House, they shall not be questioned in any other Place.

No Senator or Representative shall, during the Time for which he was elected, be appointed to any civil Office under the Authority of the United States, which shall have been created, or the Emoluments whereof shall have been encreased during such time; and no Person holding any Office under the United States, shall be a Member of either House during his Continuance in Office.

Section. 7. All Bills for raising Revenue shall originate in the House of Representatives; but the Senate may propose or concur with Amendments as on other Bills.

Every Bill which shall have passed the House of Representatives and the Senate, shall, before it become a Law, be presented to the President of the United States;[2] If he approve he shall sign it, but if not he shall return it, with his Objections to that House in which it shall have originated, who shall enter the Objections at large on their Journal, and proceed to reconsider it. If after such Reconsideration two thirds of that House shall agree to pass the Bill, it shall be sent, together with the Objections, to the other House, by which it shall likewise be reconsidered, and if approved by two thirds of that House, it shall become a Law. But in all such Cases the Votes of both Houses shall be determined by yeas and Nays, and the Names of the Persons voting for and against the Bill shall be entered on the Journal of each House respectively. If any Bill shall not be returned by the President within ten Days (Sundays excepted) after it shall have been presented to him, the Same shall be a Law, in like Manner as if he had signed it, unless the Congress by their Adjournment prevent its Return, in which Case it shall not be a Law.

Every Order, Resolution, or Vote to which the Concurrence of the Senate and House of Representatives may be necessary (except on a question of Adjournment) shall be presented to the President of the United States; and before the Same shall take Effect, shall be approved by him, or being disapproved by him, shall be repassed by two thirds of the Senate and House of Representatives, according to the Rules and Limitations prescribed in the Case of a Bill.

Section. 8. The Congress shall have Power To lay and collect Taxes, Duties, Imposts and Excises, to pay the Debts and provide for the common Defence and general Welfare of the United States; but all Duties, Imposts and Excises shall be uniform throughout the United States;

To borrow Money on the credit of the United States;

To regulate Commerce with foreign Nations, and among the several States, and with the Indian Tribes;

To establish an uniform Rule of Naturalization, and uniform Laws on the subject of Bankruptcies throughout the United States;

To coin Money, regulate the Value thereof, and of foreign Coin, and fix the Standard of Weights and Measures;

To provide for the Punishment of counterfeiting the Securities and current Coin of the United States;

To establish Post Offices and post Roads;

To promote the Progress of Science and useful Arts, by securing for limited Times to Authors and Inventors the exclusive Right to their respective Writings and Discoveries;

To constitute Tribunals inferior to the supreme Court;

To define and punish Piracies and Felonies committed on the high Seas, and Offences against the Law of Nations;

To declare War, grant Letters of Marque and Reprisal, and make Rules concerning Captures on Land and Water;

To raise and support Armies, but no Appropriation of Money to that Use shall be for a longer Term than two Years;

To provide and maintain a Navy;

To make Rules for the Government and Regulation of the land and naval Forces;

To provide for calling forth the Militia to execute the Laws of the Union, suppress Insurrections and repel Invasions;

To provide for organizing, arming, and disciplining, the Militia, and for governing such Part of them as may be employed in the Service of the United States, reserving to the States respectively, the Appointment of the Officers, and the Authority of training the Militia according to the discipline prescribed by Congress;

To exercise exclusive Legislation in all Cases whatsoever, over such District (not exceeding ten Miles square) as may, by Cession of particular States, and the Acceptance of Congress, become the Seat of the Government of the United States, and to exercise like Authority over all Places purchased by the Consent of the Legislature of the State in which the Same shall be, for the Erection of Forts, Magazines, Arsenals, dock-Yards, and other needful Buildings; — And

To make all Laws which shall be necessary and proper for carrying into Execution the foregoing Powers, and all other Powers vested by this Constitution in the Government of the United States, or in any Department or Officer thereof.

Section. 9. The Migration or Importation of such Persons as any of the States now existing shall think proper to admit, shall not be prohibited by the Congress prior to the Year one thousand eight hundred and eight, but a Tax or duty may be imposed on such Importation, not exceeding ten dollars for each Person.

The Privilege of the Writ of Habeas Corpus shall not be suspended, unless when in Cases of Rebellion or Invasion the public Safety may require it.

No Bill of Attainder or ex post facto Law shall be passed.

No Capitation, or other direct, Tax shall be laid, unless in Proportion to the Census or Enumeration herein before directed to be taken.

No Tax or Duty shall be laid on Articles exported from any State.

No Preference shall be given by any Regulation of Commerce or Revenue to the Ports of one State over those of another; nor shall Vessels bound to, or from, one State, be obliged to enter, clear, or pay Duties in another.

No Money shall be drawn from the Treasury, but in Consequence of Appropriations made by Law; and a regular Statement and Account of the Receipts and Expenditures of all public Money shall be published from time to time.

No Title of Nobility shall be granted by the United States: And no Person holding any Office of Profit or Trust under them, shall, without the Consent of the Congress, accept of any present, Emolument, Office, or Title, of any kind whatever, from any King, Prince, or foreign State.

Section. 10. No State shall enter into any Treaty, Alliance, or Confederation; grant Letters of Marque and Reprisal; coin Money; emit Bills of Credit; make any Thing but gold and silver Coin a Tender in Payment of Debts; pass any Bill of Attainder, ex post facto Law, or Law impairing the Obligation of Contracts, or grant any Title of Nobility.

No State shall, without the Consent of the Congress, lay any Imposts or Duties on Imports or Exports, except what may be absolutely necessary for executing it's inspection Laws; and the net Produce of all Duties and Imposts, laid by any State on Imports or Exports, shall be for the Use of the Treasury of the United States; and all such Laws shall be subject to the Revision and Controul of the Congress.

No State shall, without the Consent of Congress, lay any Duty of Tonnage, keep Troops, or Ships of War in time of Peace, enter into any Agreement or Compact with another State, or with a foreign Power, or engage in War, unless actually invaded, or in such imminent Danger as will not admit of delay.

Article II

Section. 1. The executive Power shall be vested in a President of the United States of America. He shall hold his Office during the Term of four Years, and, together with the Vice President, chosen for the same Term, be elected, as follows:

Each State shall appoint, in such Manner as the Legislature thereof may direct, a Number of Electors, equal to the whole Number of Senators and Representatives to which the State may be entitled in the Congress: but no Senator or Representative, or Person holding an Office of Trust or Profit under the United States, shall be appointed an Elector.

The Electors shall meet in their respective States, and vote by Ballot for two Persons, of whom one at least shall not be an Inhabitant of the same State with themselves. And they shall make a List of all the Persons voted for, and of the Number of Votes for each; which List they shall sign and certify, and transmit sealed to the Seat of the Government of the United States, directed to the President of the Senate. The President of the Senate shall, in the Presence of the Senate and House of Representatives, open all the Certificates, and the Votes shall then be counted. The Person having the greatest Number of Votes shall be the President, if such Number be a Majority of the whole Number of Electors appointed; and if there be more than one who have such Majority, and have an equal Number of Votes, then the House of Representatives shall immediately chuse by Ballot one of them for President; and if no Person have a Majority, then from the five highest on the List the said House shall in like Manner chuse the President. But in chusing the

President, the Votes shall be taken by States, the Representation from each State having one Vote; a quorum for this Purpose shall consist of a Member or Members from two thirds of the States, and a Majority of all the States shall be necessary to a Choice. In every Case, after the Choice of the President, the Person having the greatest Number of Votes of the Electors shall be the Vice President. But if there should remain two or more who have equal Votes, the Senate shall chuse from them by Ballot the Vice President [Modified by Amendment XII].

The Congress may determine the Time of chusing the Electors, and the Day on which they shall give their Votes; which Day shall be the same throughout the United States.

No Person except a natural born Citizen, or a Citizen of the United States, at the time of the Adoption of this Constitution, shall be eligible to the Office of President; neither shall any Person be eligible to that Office who shall not have attained to the Age of thirty five Years, and been fourteen Years a Resident within the United States.

In Case of the Removal of the President from Office, or of his Death, Resignation, or Inability to discharge the Powers and Duties of the said Office, the Same shall devolve on the Vice President, and the Congress may by Law provide for the Case of Removal, Death, Resignation or Inability, both of the President and Vice President, declaring what Officer shall then act as President, and such Officer shall act accordingly, until the Disability be removed, or a President shall be elected [Modified by Amendment XXV].

The President shall, at stated Times, receive for his Services, a Compensation, which shall neither be increased nor diminished during the Period for which he shall have been elected, and he shall not receive within that Period any other Emolument from the United States, or any of them.

Before he enter on the Execution of his Office, he shall take the following Oath or Affirmation: — "I do solemnly swear (or affirm) that I will faithfully execute the Office of President of the United States, and will to the best of my Ability, preserve, protect and defend the Constitution of the United States."

Section. 2. The President shall be Commander in Chief of the Army and Navy of the United States, and of the Militia of the several States, when called into the actual Service of the United States; he may require the Opinion, in writing, of the principal Officer in each of the executive Departments, upon any Subject relating to the Duties of their respective Offices, and he shall have Power to grant Reprieves and Pardons for Offences against the United States, except in Cases of Impeachment.

He shall have Power, by and with the Advice and Consent of the Senate, to make Treaties, provided two thirds of the Senators present concur; and he shall nominate, and by and with the Advice and Consent of the Senate, shall appoint Ambassadors, other public Ministers and Consuls, Judges of the supreme Court, and all other Officers of the United States, whose Appointments are not herein otherwise provided for, and which shall be established by Law: but the Congress may by Law vest the Appointment of such inferior Officers, as they think proper, in the President alone, in the Courts of Law, or in the Heads of Departments.

The President shall have Power to fill up all Vacancies that may happen during the Recess of the Senate, by granting Commissions which shall expire at the End of their next Session.

Section. 3. He shall from time to time give to the Congress Information of the State of the Union, and recommend to their Consideration such Measures as he shall judge necessary and expedient; he may, on extraordinary Occasions, convene both Houses, or either of them, and in Case of Disagreement between them, with Respect to the Time of Adjournment, he may adjourn them to such Time as he shall think proper; he shall receive Ambassadors and other public Ministers; he shall take Care that the Laws be faithfully executed, and shall Commission all the Officers of the United States.

Section. 4. The President, Vice President and all civil Officers of the United States, shall be removed from Office on Impeachment for, and Conviction of, Treason, Bribery, or other high Crimes and Misdemeanors.

Article III

Section. 1. The judicial Power of the United States shall be vested in one supreme Court, and in such inferior Courts as the Congress may from time to time ordain and establish. The Judges, both of the supreme and inferior Courts, shall hold their Offices during good Behaviour, and shall, at stated Times, receive for their Services a Compensation, which shall not be diminished during their Continuance in Office.

Section. 2. The judicial Power shall extend to all Cases, in Law and Equity, arising under this Constitution, the Laws of the United States, and Treaties made, or which shall be made, under their Authority; — to all Cases affecting Ambassadors, other public Ministers and Consuls; — to all Cases of admiralty and maritime Jurisdiction; — to Controversies to which the United States shall be a Party; — to Controversies between two or more States; — *between a State and Citizens of another State* [Modified by Amendment XI]; — between Citizens of different States; — between Citizens of the same State claiming Lands under Grants of different States, and between a State, or the Citizens thereof, and foreign States, Citizens or Subjects.

In all Cases affecting Ambassadors, other public Ministers and Consuls, and those in which a State shall be Party, the supreme Court shall have original Jurisdiction. In all the other Cases before mentioned, the supreme Court shall have appellate Jurisdiction, both as to Law and Fact, with such Exceptions, and under such Regulations as the Congress shall make.

The Trial of all Crimes, except in Cases of Impeachment, shall be by Jury; and such Trial shall be held in the State where the said Crimes shall have been committed; but when not committed within any State, the Trial shall be at such Place or Places as the Congress may by Law have directed.

Section. 3. Treason against the United States shall consist only in levying War against them, or in adhering to their Enemies, giving them Aid and Comfort. No Person shall be convicted of Treason unless on the Testimony of two Witnesses to the same overt Act, or on Confession in open Court.

The Congress shall have Power to declare the Punishment of Treason, but no Attainder of Treason shall work Corruption of Blood, or Forfeiture except during the Life of the Person attainted.

Article IV

Section. 1. Full Faith and Credit shall be given in each State to the public Acts, Records, and judicial Proceedings of every other State. And the Congress may by general Laws prescribe the Manner in which such Acts, Records and Proceedings shall be proved, and the Effect thereof.

Section. 2. The Citizens of each State shall be entitled to all Privileges and Immunities of Citizens in the several States.

A Person charged in any State with Treason, Felony, or other Crime, who shall flee from Justice, and be found in another State, shall on Demand of the executive Authority of the State from which he fled, be delivered up, to be removed to the State having Jurisdiction of the Crime.

No Person held to Service or Labour in one State, under the Laws thereof, escaping into another, shall, in Consequence of any Law or Regulation therein, be discharged from such Service or Labour, but shall be delivered up on Claim of the Party to whom such Service or Labour may be due [Modified by Amendment XIII].

Section. 3. New States may be admitted by the Congress into this Union; but no new State shall be formed or erected within the Jurisdiction of any other State; nor any State be formed by the Junction of two or more States, or

Parts of States, without the Consent of the Legislatures of the States concerned as well as of the Congress.

The Congress shall have Power to dispose of and make all needful Rules and Regulations respecting the Territory or other Property belonging to the United States; and nothing in this Constitution shall be so construed as to Prejudice any Claims of the United States, or of any particular State.

Section. 4. The United States shall guarantee to every State in this Union a Republican Form of Government, and shall protect each of them against Invasion; and on Application of the Legislature, or of the Executive (when the Legislature cannot be convened), against domestic Violence.

Article V

The Congress, whenever two thirds of both Houses shall deem it necessary, shall propose Amendments to this Constitution, or, on the Application of the Legislatures of two thirds of the several States, shall call a Convention for proposing Amendments, which, in either Case, shall be valid to all Intents and Purposes, as Part of this Constitution, when ratified by the Legislatures of three fourths of the several States, or by Conventions in three fourths thereof, as the one or the other Mode of Ratification may be proposed by the Congress; Provided that no Amendment which may be made prior to the Year One thousand eight hundred and eight shall in any Manner affect the first and fourth Clauses in the Ninth Section of the first Article; *and that no State, without its Consent, shall be deprived of its equal Suffrage in the Senate.*

Article VI

All Debts contracted and Engagements entered into, before the Adoption of this Constitution, shall be as valid against the United States under this Constitution, as under the Confederation.

This Constitution, and the Laws of the United States which shall be made in Pursuance thereof; and all Treaties made, or which shall be made, under the Authority of the United States, shall be the supreme Law of the Land; and the Judges in every State shall be bound thereby, any Thing in the Constitution or Laws of any State to the Contrary notwithstanding.

The Senators and Representatives before mentioned, and the Members of the several State Legislatures, and all executive and judicial Officers, both of the United States and of the several States, shall be bound by Oath or Affirmation, to support this Constitution; but no religious Test shall ever be required as a Qualification to any Office or public Trust under the United States.

Article VII

The Ratification of the Conventions of nine States, shall be sufficient for the Establishment of this Constitution between the States so ratifying the Same.

Done in Convention by the Unanimous Consent of the States present the Seventeenth Day of September in the Year of our Lord one thousand seven hundred and Eighty seven and of the Independance of the United States of America the Twelfth In witness whereof We have hereunto subscribed our Names,

Attest William Jackson

Secretary

done in Convention by the Unanimous Consent of the States present the Seventeenth Day of September in the Year of our Lord one thousand seven hundred and Eighty seven and of the Independence of the United States of America the Twelfth In witness whereof We have hereunto subscribed our Names,

G_o. WASHINGTON — Presid_t and deputy from Virginia

Delaware

GEO: READ

GUNNING BEDFORD jun

JOHN DICKINSON

RICHARD BASSETT

JACO: BROOM

Maryland

JAMES MCHENRY

DAN OF ST THOS. JENIFER

DANL CARROLL

Virginia

JOHN BLAIR

JAMES MADISON Jr.

North Carolina

WM. BLOUNT

RICHD. DOBBS SPAIGHT

HU WILLIAMSON

South Carolina

J. RUTLEDGE

CHARLES COTESWORTH PINCKNEY

CHARLES PINCKNEY

PIERCE BUTLER

Georgia

WILLIAM FEW

ABR BALDWIN

New Hampshire

JOHN LANGDON

NICHOLAS GILMAN

Massachusetts

NATHANIEL GORHAM

RUFUS KING

Connecticut

WM. SAML. JOHNSON

ROGER SHERMAN

New York

A<small>LEXANDER</small> H<small>AMILTON</small>

New Jersey

W<small>IL</small>: L<small>IVINGSTON</small>

D<small>AVID</small> B<small>REARLEY</small>.

W<small>M</small>. P<small>ATERSON</small>.

J<small>ONA</small>: D<small>AYTON</small>

Pennsylvania

B F<small>RANKLIN</small>

T<small>HOMAS</small> M<small>IFFLIN</small>

R<small>OBT</small> M<small>ORRIS</small>

G<small>EO</small>. C<small>LYMER</small>

T<small>HOS</small>. F<small>ITZ</small> S<small>IMONS</small>

J<small>ARED</small> I<small>NGERSOLL</small>

J<small>AMES</small> W<small>ILSON</small>

G<small>OUV</small> M<small>ORRIS</small>

In Convention Monday, September 17th, 1787.

Present

The States of

New Hampshire, Massachusetts, Connecticut, Mʀ. Hamilton from New York, New Jersey, Pennsylvania, Delaware, Maryland, Virginia, North Carolina, South Carolina and Georgia.

Resolved,

That the preceeding Constitution be laid before the United States in Congress assembled, and that it is the Opinion of this Convention, that it should afterwards be submitted to a Convention of Delegates, chosen in each State by the People thereof, under the Recommendation of its Legislature, for their Assent and Ratification; and that each Convention assenting to, and ratifying the Same, should give Notice thereof to the United States in Congress assembled. Resolved, That it is the Opinion of this Convention, that as soon as the Conventions of nine States shall have ratified this Constitution, the United States in Congress assembled should fix a Day on which Electors should be appointed by the States which have ratified the same, and a Day on which the Electors should assemble to vote for the President, and the Time and Place for commencing Proceedings under this Constitution. That after such Publication the Electors should be appointed, and the Senators and Representatives elected: That the Electors should meet on the Day fixed for the Election of the President, and should transmit their Votes certified, signed, sealed and directed, as the Constitution requires, to the Secretary of the United States in Congress assembled, that the Senators and Representatives should convene at the Time and Place assigned; that the Senators should appoint a President of the Senate, for the sole purpose of receiving, opening and counting the Votes for President; and, that after he shall be chosen, the Congress, together with the President, should, without Delay, proceed to execute this Constitution.

By the Unanimous Order of the Convention

G_o. WASHINGTON — Presid_{t.}

W. JACKSON Secretary.

The First Ten Amendments – The Bill of Rights

Ratified 1791

Amendment I

Congress shall make no law respecting an establishment of religion, or prohibiting the free exercise thereof; or abridging the freedom of speech, or of the press; or the right of the people peaceably to assemble, and to petition the Government for a redress of grievances.

Amendment II

A well regulated Militia, being necessary to the security of a free State, the right of the people to keep and bear Arms, shall not be infringed.

Amendment III

No Soldier shall, in time of peace be quartered in any house, without the consent of the Owner, nor in time of war, but in a manner to be prescribed by law.

Amendment IV

The right of the people to be secure in their persons, houses, papers, and effects, against unreasonable searches and seizures, shall not be violated, and no Warrants shall issue, but upon probable cause, supported by Oath or affirmation, and particularly describing the place to be searched, and the persons or things to be seized.

Amendment V

No person shall be held to answer for a capital, or otherwise infamous crime, unless on a presentment or indictment of a Grand Jury, except in cases arising in the land or naval forces, or in the Militia, when in actual service in time of War or public danger; nor shall any person be subject for the same offence to be twice put in jeopardy of life or limb; nor shall be compelled in any criminal case to be a witness against himself, nor be deprived of life, liberty, or property, without due process of law; nor shall private property be taken for public use, without just compensation.

Amendment VI

In all criminal prosecutions, the accused shall enjoy the right to a speedy and public trial, by an impartial jury of the State and district wherein the crime shall have been committed, which district shall have been previously ascertained by law, and to be informed of the nature and cause of the accusation; to be confronted with the witnesses against him; to have compulsory process for obtaining witnesses in his favor, and to have the Assistance of Counsel for his defence.

Amendment VII

In Suits at common law, where the value in controversy shall exceed twenty dollars, the right of trial by jury shall be preserved, and no fact tried by a jury, shall be otherwise re-examined in any Court of the United States, than according to the rules of the common law.

Amendment VIII

Excessive bail shall not be required, nor excessive fines imposed, nor cruel and unusual punishments inflicted.

Amendment IX

The enumeration in the Constitution, of certain rights, shall not be construed to deny or disparage others retained by the people.

Amendment X

The powers not delegated to the United States by the Constitution, nor prohibited by it to the States, are reserved to the States respectively, or to the people.

Additional Amendments to the Constitution

ARTICLES in addition to, and Amendment of, the Constitution of the United States of America, proposed by Congress, and ratified by the Legislatures of the several States, pursuant to the fifth Article of the original Constitution.

Amendment XI
[Proposed 1794; Ratified 1798]

The Judicial power of the United States shall not be construed to extend to any suit in law or equity, commenced or prosecuted against one of the United States by Citizens of another State, or by Citizens or Subjects of any Foreign State.

Amendment XII
[Proposed 1803; Ratified 1804]

The Electors shall meet in their respective states, and vote by ballot for President and Vice-President, one of whom, at least, shall not be an inhabitant of the same state with themselves; they shall name in their ballots the person voted for as President, and in distinct ballots the person voted for as Vice-President, and they shall make distinct lists of all persons voted for as President, and of all persons voted for as Vice-President, and of the number of votes for each, which lists they shall sign and certify, and transmit sealed to the seat of the government of the United States, directed to the President of the Senate; — The President of the Senate shall, in the presence of the Senate and House of Representatives, open all the certificates and the votes shall then be counted; — The person having the greatest number of votes for President, shall be the President, if such number be a majority of the whole number of Electors appointed; and if no person have such majority, then from the persons having the highest numbers not exceeding three on the list of those voted for as President, the House of Representatives shall choose immediately, by ballot, the President. But in choosing the President, the votes shall be taken by states, the representation from each state having one vote; a quorum for this purpose shall consist of a member or members from two-thirds of the states, and a majority of all the states shall be necessary to a choice. And if the House of Representatives shall not choose a President whenever the right of choice shall devolve upon them, before the fourth day of March next following, then the Vice-President shall act as President, as in the case of the death or other constitutional disability of the President. — The person having the greatest number of votes as Vice-President, shall be the Vice-President, if such number be a majority of the whole number of Electors appointed, and if no person have a majority, then from the two highest numbers on the list, the Senate shall choose the Vice-President; a quorum for the purpose shall consist of two-thirds of the whole number of Senators, and a majority of the whole number shall be necessary to a choice. But no person constitutionally ineligible to the office of President shall be eligible to that of Vice-President of the United States.

Amendment XIII
[Proposed 1865; Ratified 1865]

Section. 1. Neither slavery nor involuntary servitude, except as a punishment for crime whereof the party shall have been duly convicted, shall exist within the United States, or any place subject to their jurisdiction.

Section. 2. Congress shall have power to enforce this article by appropriate legislation.

Amendment XIV
Proposed 1866; ratified 1868

Section. 1. All persons born or naturalized in the United States, and subject to the jurisdiction thereof, are citizens of the United States and of the State wherein they reside. No State shall make or enforce any law which shall abridge the privileges or immunities of citizens of the United States; nor shall any State deprive any person of life, liberty, or property, without due process of law; nor deny to any person within its jurisdiction the equal protection of the laws.

Section. 2. Representatives shall be apportioned among the several States according to their respective numbers, counting the whole number of persons in each State, excluding Indians not taxed. But when the right to vote at any election for the choice of electors for President and Vice President of the United States, Representatives in Congress, the Executive and Judicial officers of a State, or the members of the Legislature thereof, is denied to any of the male inhabitants of such State, being twenty-one years of age, and citizens of the United States, or in any way abridged, except for participation in rebellion, or other crime, the basis of representation therein shall be reduced in the proportion which the number of such male citizens shall bear to the whole number of male citizens twenty-one years of age in such State.

Section. 3. No person shall be a Senator or Representative in Congress, or elector of President and Vice President, or hold any office, civil or military, under the United States, or under any State, who, having previously taken an oath, as a member of Congress, or as an officer of the United States, or as a member of any State legislature, or as an executive or judicial officer of any State, to support the Constitution of the United States, shall have engaged in insurrection or rebellion against the same, or given aid or comfort to the enemies thereof. But Congress may by a vote of two-thirds of each House, remove such disability.

Section. 4. The validity of the public debt of the United States, authorized by law, including debts incurred for payment of pensions and bounties for services in suppressing insurrection or rebellion, shall not be questioned. But neither the United States nor any State shall assume or pay any debt or obligation incurred in aid of insurrection or rebellion against the United States, or any claim for the loss or emancipation of any slave; but all such debts, obligations and claims shall be held illegal and void.

Section. 5. The Congress shall have power to enforce, by appropriate legislation, the provisions of this article.

Amendment XV
[Proposed 1869; Ratified 1870]

Section. 1. The right of citizens of the United States to vote shall not be denied or abridged by the United States or by any State on account of race, color, or previous condition of servitude.

Section. 2. The Congress shall have power to enforce this article by appropriate legislation.

Amendment XVI
[Proposed 1909; Ratified 1913]

The Congress shall have power to lay and collect taxes on incomes, from whatever source derived, without apportionment among the several States, and without regard to any census or enumeration.

Amendment XVII
[Proposed 1912; Ratified 1913; Possibly Unconstitutional (See Article V, Clause 3 of the Constitution)]

The Senate of the United States shall be composed of two Senators from each State, elected by the people thereof, for six years; and each Senator shall have one vote. The electors in each State shall have the qualifications requisite for electors of the most numerous branch of the State legislatures.

When vacancies happen in the representation of any State in the Senate, the executive authority of such State shall issue writs of election to fill such vacancies: Provided, That the legislature of any State may empower the executive thereof to make temporary appointments until the people fill the vacancies by election as the legislature may direct.

This amendment shall not be so construed as to affect the election or term of any Senator chosen before it becomes valid as part of the Constitution.

Amendment XVIII
[Proposed 1917; Ratified 1919; Repealed 1933
(See Amendment XXI, Section 1

Section. 1. After one year from the ratification of this article the manufacture, sale, or transportation of intoxicating liquors within, the importation thereof into, or the exportation thereof from the United States and all territory subject to the jurisdiction thereof for beverage purposes is hereby prohibited.

Section. 2. The Congress and the several States shall have concurrent power to enforce this article by appropriate legislation.

Section. 3. This article shall be inoperative unless it shall have been ratified as an amendment to the Constitution by the legislatures of the several States, as provided in the Constitution, within seven years from the date of the submission hereof to the States by the Congress.

Amendment XIX
[Proposed 1919; Ratified 1920]

The right of citizens of the United States to vote shall not be denied or abridged by the United States or by any State on account of sex.

Congress shall have power to enforce this article by appropriate legislation.

Amendment XX
[Proposed 1932; Ratified 1933]

Section. 1. The terms of the President and Vice President shall end at noon on the 20th day of January, and the terms of Senators and Representatives at noon on the

3d day of January, of the years in which such terms would have ended if this article had not been ratified; and the terms of their successors shall then begin.

Section. 2. The Congress shall assemble at least once in every year, and such meeting shall begin at noon on the 3d day of January, unless they shall by law appoint a different day.

Section. 3. If, at the time fixed for the beginning of the term of the President, the President elect shall have died, the Vice President elect shall become President. If a President shall not have been chosen before the time fixed for the beginning of his term, or if the President elect shall have failed to qualify, then the Vice President elect shall act as President until a President shall have qualified; and the Congress may by law provide for the case wherein neither a President elect nor a Vice President elect shall have qualified, declaring who shall then act as President, or the manner in which one who is to act shall be selected, and such person shall act accordingly until a President or Vice President shall have qualified.

Section. 4. The Congress may by law provide for the case of the death of any of the persons from whom the House of Representatives may choose a President whenever the right of choice shall have devolved upon them, and for the case of the death of any of the persons from whom the Senate may choose a Vice President whenever the right of choice shall have devolved upon them.

Section. 5. Sections 1 and 2 shall take effect on the 15th day of October following the ratification of this article.

Section. 6. This article shall be inoperative unless it shall have been ratified as an amendment to the Constitution by the legislatures of three-fourths of the several States within seven years from the date of its submission.

Amendment XXI
[Proposed 1933; Ratified 1933]

Section. 1. The eighteenth article of amendment to the Constitution of the United States is hereby repealed.

Section. 2. The transportation or importation into any State, Territory, or possession of the United States for delivery or use therein of intoxicating liquors, in violation of the laws thereof, is hereby prohibited.

Section. 3. This article shall be inoperative unless it shall have been ratified as an amendment to the Constitution by conventions in the several States, as provided in the Constitution, within seven years from the date of the submission hereof to the States by the Congress.

Amendment XXII
[Proposed 1947; Ratified 1951]

Section. 1. No person shall be elected to the office of the President more than twice, and no person who has held the office of President, or acted as President, for more than two years of a term to which some other person was elected President shall be elected to the office of the President more than once. But this Article shall not apply to any person holding the office of President when this Article was proposed by the Congress, and shall not prevent any person who may be holding the office of President, or acting as President, during the term within which this Article becomes operative from holding the office of President or acting as President during the remainder of such term.

Section. 2. This article shall be inoperative unless it shall have been ratified as an amendment to the Constitution by the legislatures of three-fourths of the several States within seven years from the date of its submission to the States by the Congress.

Amendment XXIII
[Proposed 1960; Ratified 1961]

Section. 1. The District constituting the seat of Government of the United States shall appoint in such manner as the Congress may direct:

A number of electors of President and Vice President equal to the whole number of Senators and Representatives in Congress to which the District would be entitled if it were a State, but in no event more than the least populous State; they shall be in addition to those appointed by the States, but they shall be considered, for the purposes of the election of President and Vice President, to be electors appointed by a State; and they shall meet in the District and perform such duties as provided by the twelfth article of amendment.

Section. 2. The Congress shall have power to enforce this article by appropriate legislation.

Amendment XXIV
[Proposed 1962; Ratified 1964]

Section. 1. The right of citizens of the United States to vote in any primary or other election for President or Vice President, for electors for President or Vice President, or for Senator or Representative in Congress, shall not be denied or abridged by the United States or any State by reason of failure to pay any poll tax or other tax.

Section. 2. The Congress shall have power to enforce this article by appropriate legislation.

Amendment XXV
[Proposed 1965; Ratified 1967]

Section. 1. In case of the removal of the President from office or of his death or resignation, the Vice President shall become President.

Section. 2. Whenever there is a vacancy in the office of the Vice President, the President shall nominate a Vice President who shall take office upon confirmation by a majority vote of both Houses of Congress.

Section. 3. Whenever the President transmits to the President pro tempore of the Senate and the Speaker of the House of Representatives his written declaration that he is unable to discharge the powers and duties of his office, and until he transmits to them a written declaration to the contrary, such powers and duties shall be discharged by the Vice President as Acting President.

Section. 4. Whenever the Vice President and a majority of either the principal officers of the executive departments or of such other body as Congress may by law provide, transmit to the President pro tempore of the Senate and the Speaker of the House of Representatives their written declaration that the President is unable to discharge the powers and duties of his office, the Vice President shall immediately assume the powers and duties of the office as Acting President.

Thereafter, when the President transmits to the President pro tempore of the Senate and the Speaker of the House of Representatives his written declaration that no inability exists, he shall resume the powers and duties of his office unless the Vice President and a majority of either the principal officers of the executive department or of such other body as Congress may by law provide, transmit within four days to the President pro tempore of the Senate and the Speaker of the House of Representatives their written declaration that the President is unable to discharge the powers and duties of his office. Thereupon Congress shall decide the issue, assembling within forty-eight hours for that purpose if not in session. If the Congress, within twenty-one days after receipt of the latter written declaration, or, if Congress is not in session, within twenty-one days after Congress is required to assemble, determines by two-thirds vote of both Houses that the President is unable to discharge the powers and duties of his office, the Vice President shall continue to discharge the same as Acting President; otherwise, the President shall resume the powers and duties of his office.

Amendment XXVI
[Proposed 1971; Ratified 1971]

Section. 1. The right of citizens of the United States, who are eighteen years of age or older, to vote shall not be denied or abridged by the United States or by any State on account of age.

Section. 2. The Congress shall have power to enforce this article by appropriate legislation.

Amendment XXVII
[Proposed 1789; Ratified 1992]

No law, varying the compensation for the services of the Senators and Representatives, shall take effect, until an election of Representatives shall have intervened.

Acknowledgements

You can write a book by yourself, but to produce a book worth reading requires the dedicated input of many people. I first wish to thank my wife Lynda. Her many years in publishing have made her an editor beyond compare. She was even kind enough to be polite when pointing to my errors. Editor Nick Wartella, for many years an English teacher, has the eye of a hawk. His many suggestions and sharp recommendations have humbled me. My friend of many years, Ken Taub, lent me his eyes and mind and made a tremendous contribution to the book. A published author himself, Ken brought to bear his many years as an advertising executive. And finally, James K. O'Sullivan, my friend, former colleague, and successful appellate attorney combed through the book with the critical substantive eye of a fellow attorney. Jim's comments have been invaluable.

About the Author

Russell F. Moran is an attorney admitted in New York State and the Federal courts of New York. He graduated from Chicago-Kent Law School, where he attended with a full academic scholarship and served as an editor of the Chicago Kent Law Review. In his senior year he tought legal research and writing. He was founder and editor-in-chief of *The New York Jury Verdict Reporter*, incorporated as Moran Publishing Company, Inc. which was sold to American Lawyer Media in 2000. The company also published *Judicial Review of Damages*, a monthly that published what happens to jury verdicts on appeal, and the *Civil, Criminal, Matrimonial and Tort Citators*, books that were updated quarterly and are used by lawyers to prepare motions and appeals. He served as a District Court Arbitrator in Suffolk County New York. He has appeared on TV and radio, and has been quoted in numerous publications on jury trends, including the Op-Ed page of the *New York Times*.